Building Capacity through Financial Management

A Practical Guide

Oxfam GB

Oxfam GB, founded in 1942, is a development, humanitarian, and campaigning agency dedicated to finding lasting solutions to poverty and suffering around the world. Oxfam believes that every human being is entitled to a life of dignity and opportunity, and it works with others worldwide to make this become a reality.

From its base in Oxford in the United Kingdom, Oxfam GB publishes and distributes a wide range of books and other resource materials for development and relief workers, researchers and campaigners, schools and colleges, and the general public, as part of its programme of advocacy, education, and communications.

Oxfam GB is a member of Oxfam International, a confederation of 13 agencies of diverse cultures and languages, which share a commitment to working for an end to injustice and poverty – both in long-term development work and at times of crisis.

For further information about Oxfam's publishing, and online ordering, visit www.oxfam.org.uk/publications

For information about Oxfam's development, advocacy, and humanitarian relief work around the world, visit www.oxfam.org.uk

OXFAM SKILLS AND PRACTICE

Books in this series offer practical guidelines for development and humanitarian practitioners. Based on Oxfam's programme experience, they are designed to consolidate and share learning, and encourage good practice. Below is a list of recent titles in the series. For a full and up-to-date listing see our website: www.oxfam.org.uk/publications

Cash-Transfer Programming in Emergencies
by Pantaleo Creti and Susanne Jaspars, 2006

Effective Consultancies in Development and Humanitarian Programmes
by John Rowley and Frances Rubin, 2006

Producer Organisations: A Guide to Developing Collective Rural Enterprises
by Chris Penrose-Buckley, 2007

Building Capacity through Financial Management

A Practical Guide

John Cammack

Front cover (left to right)

Agir Autrement pour le Développement en Afrique, Ziguinchor, Senegal: developing the skills of finance staff. (John Cammack)

Khation Region, Tajikistan: assessments being carried out by Oxfam staff members as part of a Community Situation Indicators project. (Karen Robinson/Oxfam)

Ampara District, Sri Lanka: a workshop organised by Oxfam partner organisation AWF (Affected Women's Forum) in Thampattai camp. (Howard Davis/Oxfam)

Spine

Mali, West Africa: Bouna Baby, headmaster of Taboye School, which has received support from Oxfam's partner organisation ADESAH. (Crispen Hughes/Oxfam)

Back cover

Guatemala: interview with local man about how Oxfam partner organisation Defensor'a Maya has helped resolve land-rights issues. (Annie Bungeroth/Oxfam)

First published by Oxfam GB in 2007

ISBN 978-0-85598-576-9

A catalogue record for this publication is available from the British Library.

Available from:

Bournemouth English Book Centre, PO Box 1496, Parkstone, Dorset, BH12 3YD, UK
tel: +44 (0)1202 712933; fax: +44 (0)1202 712930; email: oxfam@bebc.co.uk

USA: Stylus Publishing LLC, PO Box 605, Herndon, VA 20172-0605, USA
tel: +1 (0)703 661 1581; fax: +1 (0)703 661 1547; email: styluspub@aol.com

For details of local agents and representatives in other countries, consult our website:
www.oxfam.org.uk/publications or contact
Oxfam Publishing, Oxfam House, John Smith Drive, Cowley, Oxford, OX4 2JY, UK
tel +44 (0) 1865 472255; fax (0) 1865 472393; email: publish@oxfam.org.uk

Our website contains a fully searchable database of all our titles, and facilities for secure on-line ordering.

Published by Oxfam GB, Oxfam House, John Smith Drive, Cowley, Oxford, OX4 2JY, UK

Printed by Information Press, Eynsham

Oxfam GB is a registered charity, no. 202 918, and is a member of Oxfam International.

Contents

List of boxes

List of figures

List of tables

Acknowledgements

Many people have helped in the preparation for this book, and I acknowledge my debt to them. In particular, I thank the Oxfam Publishing Team: Alison Beaumont, Julie Jones, Kevan Ray, and Jackie Smith. Thanks also to those who have read through and provided comments on earlier drafts of the text: Adeola Akintoye, Freda Cammack, Stephen Cammack, John Cropper, Jacques Lauruol, Julieanne Porter, and Gopal Rao.

I am grateful to many people and organisations for help with the research, including Adeola Akintoye, Paul Anticoni, Mark Awiah, Jo Baker, Phan Kunthak Botum, Westone Mutale Bowa, Bill Bruty, Jo Burton, Ken Carleton, Chilmba ChiyeÀu, Mohammed Coulibaly, Ndeye Marie Fall Diagne, Abdoul Ma Ali Diallo, Tacko Sy Diop, Sally East, Nicola Elliott, Janey Forgan, Sharda Ganga, Clive Gillam, Bronwyn Harris, Begay Jabang, Sheeraz Ahmed Khan, Dennis Khangalani, Jacques Lauruol, Maren Lieberum, Harvey Livingston, Amédée Marescot, Aminulhaq Mayel, Alvin Mchemba, Lingalireni Mihowa, Gary Mitchell, Tendayi Moabi, San Moller, Besinati Mpepo, Dennis Mulenga, Muthoni Muriu, Samuel Musa, Clever Musonda, Felix Muyaso, Ayanda Mvimbi, Evelyn Naraga, Grace Nkhuwa, Alick Nyirenda, Mark Nyungula, Stephen Okafor, Vich Onn, Ousmane Pam, Sanjay Patra, Emma Porteous, Bryan Rambharos, Gopal Rao, Dorte Rasmussen, Mom Riam, Ernest Sessanga, Janet Shapiro, Emily Joy Sikazwe, Shamila Singh, Hang Sophearyn, Clare Syanjelele, and Roque Yap.

Contributing organisations include Afrique-Enjeux, Agir Autrement pour le Développement en Afrique, Amicale Socio-Economique Sportive et Culturelle des Agriculteurs du Walo, Amnesty International, Asylum Welcome, British Overseas NGOs for Development, British Red Cross Society, CECI Senegal, Centre for the Study of Violence and Reconciliation, Christian Aid, Cini Asha, Civil Society for Poverty

Reduction, Copperbelt Health Education Project, Dan Church Aid, Evangelical Lutheran Development Services, FAMSA Welkom, Financial Management Service Foundation, Oxfam America, Matindi Youth Organisation, Micro-Bankers Trust, PINORD, SCIAF, SOS Sahel, Stichting Projekta Surinam, VSO, Women for Change, and the Oxfam offices in Afghanistan, Cambodia, Haiti, Malawi, Philippines, Senegal, South Africa, and Zambia.

I also thank those who have participated in courses and workshops that I have facilitated, and organisations that I have visited as a consultant. Much of what I have learned from their combined wisdom is distilled throughout this book.

Last but not least, I thank Freda Cammack for her constant help and support in the process of writing this book.

John Cammack
Oxford, July 2007

Introduction

Building capacity through financial management is a key way of achieving a more effective organisation. This then leads to an improved programme of activities. With strong financial management capacity, the group or organisation becomes more able to control its own affairs. Without it, the future is often uncertain: it may be impossible to predict when money will be short and, crucially, it may become impossible to fund programmes.

This book presents practical ways to build financial management capacity in an international development context (although much of it applies to any non-profit organisation). It describes best practice in the specific tasks of financial management – for example, planning and budgeting and financial controls. It gives examples of how groups and organisations build their own capacity. It also considers what leadership teams can do to guide their organisation's long-term direction (an activity sometimes called 'governance') and it describes other financial management aspects that can be built into an organisation's structure.

It is written for non-government organisations (NGOs), larger community-based organisations (CBOs), and charities. For organisations with established systems, it provides challenging questions, both for their own organisation and for the way in which they work with others. It is hoped that the book will be used by chairs and members of management committees, leaders, directors, managers, programme staff, administrators, and finance staff. It is a tool for large NGOs and donors working with their partner CBOs and NGOs. The content can also be used in training courses.

Building stronger financial management capacity is not difficult. If you follow the suggestions in this book, you should quickly start to see the impact. Your organisation will be in a better position to show accountability, transparency, and credibility – all of which are conditions that donors consider priorities when funding programmes.

This is primarily a book about building capacity, rather than how to do accounting. Books that cover the technical aspects are listed in the 'Further reading' section. Some of the resources used in the book are freely available at www.johncammack.net (click on 'Resources').

Part 1 | Linking Capacity-Building and Finance

1 | Capacity-building and finance

This chapter considers the link between capacity-building and finance and offers some principles to guide organisations in building their own capacity. We will consider whose capacity can be built, what this means for organisations of various sizes, and some of the challenges that confront them.

Building financial management capacity is a way of providing and maintaining an infrastructure. It can be the 'scaffolding' upon which to build the rest of the organisation. If it is strong, the organisation can flourish; if not, the organisation may struggle or even collapse.

At one level, some basic financial skills are essential in order to keep accounting records and provide financial information that is required by law. But if financial management skills are used throughout the organisation, they can in addition lead to empowered staff, improved sustainability, and better programme quality and impact.

It is not difficult for a group or organisation to strengthen their financial management capacity, and it is not necessary to have an accountant in order to achieve it. Non-finance people, such as leaders, managers, and programme staff, can do this. The main tools are introduced in this book. By using them, you will start to see the impact. And you will create a model to pass on to beneficiaries, communities, or partner organisations.

Everyone arrived expectantly for the annual meeting of Salud, an organisation dedicated to caring for people living with HIV and AIDS. Clients, members, staff, volunteers, and donors all agreed that it had been an excellent year, and they looked forward to hearing about future plans.

The meeting progressed with the usual business of reports and appointing the new committee. The annual review was very positive. Several of Salud's clients told their own stories, which were moving and inspirational. Later on a client asked: 'Why are you so effective at what you do? Everyone knows Salud has excellent staff and volunteers, but is there some other magic ingredient?'

The chair looked around the room and said: 'Our founders had a vision of what we could do, and they and others have worked passionately to achieve it. A few years ago we were in serious trouble. We got to a point where no donors wanted to fund us; morale was low, and our work was starting to suffer. Donors told us that they liked our programme but said they wouldn't fund us, because we had poor financial systems. This gave us a shock, and we knew we had to improve. It hasn't been difficult for us to introduce better systems, once we grasped the basic ideas.

'So, the "magic" is the passion for our work and our strong financial management. Now we don't have problems finding donors, and our programme decisions benefit enormously from up-to-date financial information. This is what allows us to keep on supporting people living with HIV and AIDS so effectively.'

An approach to capacity-building

What is capacity-building?

'A systematic strengthening of the capabilities of an organisation to perform its mission more effectively.'[1]

The Environmental Support Center and Innovation Network identify nine principles[2] for building capacity. These principles could be expressed as shown overleaf.

1. **Every organisation is capable of building its own capacity**
   It is very important to recognise that an organisation is in charge of its own capacity-building, and that its needs are unique. This gives better results.

2. **Trust between the organisation and the capacity-builder is essential**
   Trust is at the centre of this relationship. The more trust there is, the more effective are these nine principles. Trust makes it acceptable to communicate openly, to risk disapproval, and to learn.

3. **An organisation must be ready for capacity-building**
   Organisations can benefit from capacity-building at all stages of their life. To be ready for capacity-building, an organisation needs to be
   - open to change and willing to question itself;
   - able to describe its mission clearly;
   - willing to believe that capacity-building will further its mission;
   - prepared to commit time and resources.

4. **On-going questioning means better answers**
   The most successful capacity-builders keep on asking questions, welcome feedback, and encourage change. These create a climate where true understanding is welcome, not avoided.

5. **Team and peer learning are effective capacity-building tools**
   Individuals and teams are essential for capacity-building. Facilitators may bring good ideas, but they don't have all the answers, although they can add greater momentum to the process.

6. **Capacity-building should allow for different learning styles**
   People learn in many different ways: some by doing, some by listening, some by talking, some by experimenting. Some think more visually, some more verbally. Good capacity-building recognises and uses these differences.

7. **Every organisation has its own history and culture**
   Understand and use the mission, the organisational culture, and the environment of an organisation. The more an organisation's context is understood, the more powerful the capacity-building.

8. **All the people and parts of an organisation are linked together**
   Understanding or changing an organisation is much more likely to succeed if it involves people at different levels: staff, users, committee members.

9. **Capacity-building takes time**
   Capacity-building that takes time is more likely to be absorbed into the organisation's on-going work. But short-term inputs, for example strengthening a particular skill, are also valuable.

These principles can be applied to all types of capacity-building, including financial management capacity-building. If improvements are to be sustainable, it is particularly important to remember that financial management capacity must be developed across every part of an organisation. If it is developed only with finance people, it will not be enough.

Whose financial management capacity is being built?

There are four key groups who will benefit from financial management capacity-building:

- members of the management committee
- the leader and managers
- non-finance and programme people
- finance people.

What is a management committee?

The group of people, usually volunteers, who lead a non-profit organisation and are responsible for it. In large organisations, its members may represent different parts of the organisation, meeting regularly to take policy decisions. In small groups, the management-committee role may be taken by the whole group meeting together. Whatever the size, there is likely to be a leader or chair, someone who looks after financial matters, and at least one or two other members. The committee members need to be aware of, and responsible for, the organisation's financial well-being, and they should be accountable to its stakeholders for it.

It is important to make sure that everyone is considered when assessing individuals' needs for financial management capacity-building, both in organisations and in community groups. Questions to ask include the following:

- Are those without formal qualifications included, when they have other relevant experience?
- Are women and men considered equally?
- Is training offered only to people who can read and write, ignoring those who work verbally?
- Are some groups ignored, for example people who are very poor, or older people, or those who have a disability?

Organisations of various sizes

Different-sized organisations need financial skills appropriate for their size, history, culture, context, and geographical setting.

- **Voluntary groups** with no paid staff or donor funding may need only a simple budget, a few accounting records, and some basic financial controls, for example making sure that two people sign cheques. They will not need complex systems.

- **Small to medium-sized organisations** with paid staff, premises, and maybe one or two donors will need a more developed budget, good financial controls, and accurate accounting records which can provide information to donors in the format that they need. They may employ an administrator for day-to-day transactions and a professional accountant for putting the end-of-year accounts together. Some form of annual audit helps to build their financial management capacity and gives donors confidence in them.

- **Medium to large organisations** with more paid staff, their own premises, and many donors need well-developed accounting and financial systems, possibly a computerised accounting package, experienced accounting staff, and professional annual audits.

- **Large organisations** need well-developed financial systems, professional accounting staff, an organisational budget to which donors contribute, and a full audit.

Not all groups or organisations grow in size; but if they do, their financial needs will change. Part of the task of financial management capacity-building is to identify when the next stage of development has been reached. Each organisation is different. If the number of activities increases, for example when a donor offers a large amount of funding, it is worth assessing whether the financial management capacity is adequate before accepting the money. Organisations need careful management to avoid growing too quickly for their available capacity.

Appendix A offers a guide to the minimum financial requirements needed at different points in an organisation's development.

Challenges of financial management capacity-building

Building financial management capacity can bring enormous benefits to an organisation, but it is a challenging process. It takes time to develop a full understanding of how each organisation works.

Resources are not always available, so concentrate on ways of building financial management capacity that do not require high additional costs (see Chapter 11 for some suggestions). Make it a part of your ongoing work (there are suggestions for this throughout the book). Sometimes two organisations can help each other with no cost involved. If there are costs, for example the costs of providing staff training, plan these in advance and discuss funding with donors.

When building any sort of capacity, it is important to be sure that the changes are 'embedded' into the organisation as a whole. For example, make sure that more than one person is involved, and encourage people to write down their new ways of working, as part of a simple procedure. If only one individual is developed, he or she may, having been trained, decide to leave, and the organisation will be no further forward.

When a donor is funding capacity-building, an organisation may not know how long its commitment is likely to last, and whether the funding will continue. Make sure that your organisation itself 'owns' the capacity being built, so that any change of donor has less impact. The organisation should be continually preparing itself for the eventual departure of each donor.

2 | Assessing financial management capacity

In this chapter we consider how to assess an organisation's financial management capacity in the key tasks of planning and budgeting, accounts record-keeping, financial reporting, and financial controls. We also look at external audits and other organisational aspects that influence financial management capacity.

Assessing and building financial management capacity is one of many roles that leaders, managers, programme staff, and volunteers perform. It is often part of the broader organisational capacity-building. People often recognise that an organisation has weak financial skills, but find it difficult to identify what the actual problem is and where it lies. To start to build, we need a structure to help us to decide where best to focus our efforts. A key question to consider is '*Where are the gaps between what is actually done and what should be done?*' You can then identify how these gaps can be filled.

The four specific tasks of financial management

The Campaign for Female Education (CAMFED) say that, 'Programme, sound financial management and effective community development go hand-in-hand'.[3]

What is financial management?

The use of financial information, skills, and methods to make the best use of an organisation's resources.

Financial management is making sure that an organisation manages its resources well. The four specific tasks shown in Figure 1 are the starting point for assessing and building financial management capacity. If you want to assess an organisation, there are a number of questions in each section, which, together with your knowledge about the organisation, help to build a good overview.

Figure 1: Specific tasks of strong financial management

Planning and budgeting

The management committee and managers decide their objectives for the year and forecast the cost of achieving them. This is the annual budget. As the year progresses, the management committee and managers compare actual performance with budget forecasts. They can then decide whether any action is needed – for example, to increase or decrease spending, or undertake more fundraising. This regular monitoring of the budget also helps to manage donor funding and reporting.

Questions for your organisation

- Are organisational objectives the starting point for the planning and budgeting process?
- Do the leader and management committee regularly compare budgeted income and expenditure with the actual income and expenditure, and take action where necessary, especially when donor funding is affected?
- Is there always enough money to pay for salaries, goods, and services?

Accounts record-keeping

A group or organisation must keep accurate accounting records and up-to-date records of transactions. These are the basis of the information needed to manage the organisation, and they will be used for internal and external financial reports.

Questions for your organisation

- Is the record of money coming in and going out (sometimes called 'the cash/bank book') up to date and accurate?
- Is there a separate register to record loans or other money given to staff?
- Are there documents (for example invoices and receipts) for every transaction?

Financial reporting

Financial reporting includes producing the annual accounting statements and reporting to beneficiaries, the donors, and (if necessary) the government.

Questions for your organisation

- Is it possible to identify funds that have been given for a particular purpose?
- Are financial reports submitted on time to donors?
- Are annual accounting statements produced?

Financial controls

The management committee and managers are responsible for financial controls which protect property and equipment and minimise the possibility of error and theft – for example, a system for authorising expenditure when a purchase is made. Finance staff can advise on which controls to introduce, but the leadership team must make sure that the controls are working effectively.

Questions for your organisation

- Are at least two people involved in transactions, for example authorising payments and signing the cheques?
- Are the organisation's bank figures agreed with the bank statements at least monthly? (This is sometimes called a 'bank reconciliation'.)
- Does someone, other than the person responsible for the cash, count it regularly?

External audit

Audit is an annual independent review which tests (among other things) whether the four specific tasks of financial management are working effectively. It is an excellent way of building strong financial management capacity.

Questions for your organisation

- Is there an audit/independent examination each year?
- Does the auditor make written recommendations?
- Are the auditor's recommendations prioritised and implemented?

The answers to all these questions should be 'yes'. If the answers are 'no', you should think about what is needed to build financial management capacity in that area.

Organisational aspects of financial management

The four specific tasks of financial management and external audit are not enough on their own. There are wider organisational aspects which will help you to run your organisation professionally and build strong financial management capacity. These organisational aspects, shown in Figure 2, are essential for improving the organisation's management and programme effectiveness.

Figure 2: Ingredients of strong financial management capacity

- Specific tasks
- Organisational aspects

ORGANISATIONAL CULTURE

The leadership team promote and prioritise the financial side of the organisation

Financially aware programme and non-finance staff

EXTERNAL RELATIONSHIPS

Awareness of what could go wrong

EXTERNAL AUDIT

Planning and budgeting

Financial reporting

Strong relationships eg. donors, beneficiaries

User-friendly financial systems

Strong financial management capacity

Accounts record-keeping

Financial controls

Suitably experienced finance person

Up-to-date financial management information

FINANCIAL INFORMATION

Finance staff able to communicate with non-finance staff

Trained and competant finance staff

Members are able to understand basic financial information

MANAGEMENT COMMITTEE

FINANCE STAFF

The management committee

One member of the committee should be responsible for making sure that financial issues are considered at each meeting. Other members should be competent to ask appropriate questions about any financial information presented to them.

Questions for your organisation

- Is there one member who is responsible for financial issues?
- Can other members understand the financial information and ask appropriate questions about it?
- Does the management committee approve the annual budget?

Finance staff

In small organisations with no paid staff, the management committee's finance person does most of the financial work. Larger organisations recruit finance staff to do this. The level of staff will depend on the size and complexity of the organisation. As organisations grow, more qualified staff may be required – if, for example, funding is increased.

Questions for your organisation

- Are all finance staff competent in their work?
- Are there enough finance staff?
- Can finance people (or at least one person) communicate technical issues in a straightforward way to non-finance people?

Financial information

Whether you are using a computerised accounting system or a paper-based system, the information must be accurate and up to date. Information for a management committee does not need the same level of detail as information for a project manager who is dealing with day-to-day activities. Always present the information in a format that suits the needs of each different audience.

Questions for your organisation

- Do the management committee, the leader, and managers receive up-to-date information?
- Does the information provided contain the appropriate level of detail for the different users?
- Is the information easy to understand?

> ## What is organisational culture?
>
> Organisational culture is the values, behaviour, and attitudes shared by people within an organisation. They shape the way in which it relates internally and to its stakeholders. Culture can be described as 'the way we do things around here'.

The culture of the organisation includes the priority given to financial issues. The leader, for example, must stress the importance of finance at meetings, and set a good example by making sure that his or her personal travel-expense claims are completed on time. Other staff will follow this lead. Programme staff and other non-finance staff should have a working knowledge of finance. Visiting donors are likely to be aware of a positive or negative 'culture', and may base their funding decision on it.

Questions for your organisation

- Do the management committee and leader give positive messages about finance?
- Does the leader set an example in his/her personal accounting?
- Do programme staff and non-finance staff have a working knowledge of finance?

External relationships

Organisations should maintain good relationships and communicate openly with the people with whom they work, including beneficiaries and donors. All stakeholders need to know about the financial aspects of your organisation's activities. It is important to identify and plan for things that could go wrong: for example, the withdrawal of donor funding.

Questions for your organisation

- Is your relationship with stakeholders open and transparent?
- Are your beneficiaries and/or partners given financial information in appropriate detail and format?
- Does the planning process consider what could go wrong?

The next stage

If you answer 'no' to the questions listed above, it is a sign that financial management capacity-building may be necessary.

Having looked critically at your own group or organisation, you may find that there are areas that need improvement. Prioritise this, but plan to do it over time, rather than all at once. Start with the areas that are most important and bring in outside help, if you need it.

We will consider each area of building financial management capacity in more detail in later chapters. They will show you the key approaches needed and will offer a 'toolkit' that you might use. The Review of Financial Systems in Appendix B presents the main financial systems to show exactly where financial management capacity may need building. It is important to treat the basic questions in this chapter, and the more detailed review in the Appendix, as tools for building capacity, rather than a means of judging your organisation. The aim of these tools is to help you to improve your organisation's financial and programme capacity, and to be in a position where good management, growth, and effective fundraising are more easily achieved.

Part 2 | Building Financial Management Capacity

3 | Planning and budgeting

The chapter looks at ways to build financial management capacity through planning and budgeting – the first of the four specific tasks of financial management. We will consider best practice in planning budgets, monitoring budgets, and forecasting cash flows. Finally we ask who might need to have their budgeting capacity built.

A budget is used to forecast income and expenditure. Budgeting is a valuable tool, because it helps organisations to manage their finances and develop their financial management capacity. Even small organisations prepare a budget when applying for funding, simply because donors usually ask for one. Many also monitor actual income and expenditure against what was planned, but some do not do this systematically. Monitoring is vital, both to keep control of the money, and to be sure that donor funding is being well managed.

Organisations with one donor may have a simple budget prepared in their donor's format. Larger organisations with several donors may prepare their own budget and allocate donors' funds against different parts of their budget. Others may produce a series of donor budgets, although this makes monitoring for the whole organisation more difficult.

What is budget planning?

Budgets are planning tools. They help to express objectives in financial terms. They will cover the project period or a financial year. The budget is written down, sometimes with the help of a donor, and approved by the management committee. It is then presented to potential donors for funding.

> **What is budget monitoring?**
>
> Actual income and expenditure is compared with the budget every month
> or quarter. A report – called 'budget and actual statement', or 'variance report',
> or 'management accounts' – is produced to show the comparison for each line
> of the budget. It shows the difference between budgeted income and
> expenditure and what is actually received and spent. You need to act if you see
> under-spending or over-spending, and if you have not received all the
> expected income.

Best practice: 'top 10' principles for budgeting

- Always start with the objectives for the organisation/activity and involve
  other people. Ask the person responsible for each activity to prepare a
  budget.
- Use finance staff to provide technical advice, but not to decide priorities
  (unless it is their own budget).
- Be as realistic as possible. Add notes to the budget to show how calculations
  were made. Show whether income is 'guaranteed' or 'not yet confirmed'.
- Allow plenty of time and get approval from the management committee
  and/or donors before the start of the period/year.
- Show the agreed budget (and any alterations) to group members or staff.
  Tell them what they have to do to keep within the budget.
- If external funding is required, submit the budget (or part of it) to donors.
- Provide detailed budget-monitoring reports for those with day-to-day
  management responsibility, and a summarised report for the management
  committee.
- Monitor the budget against actual income and expenditure regularly.
  Take any necessary action. The management committee, leader, and
  managers should review these reports regularly. An example is shown
  in Table 1.
- Add notes to budget-monitoring reports, to explain major differences
  between the budget and actual income and expenditure.
- Keep donors informed of any changes to the budget (for example,
  if expenditure is more than the budget for one item and under budget
  in another).

Table 1: Example of a budget and actual statement

Southern Farmers' Support Organisation
Budget and Actual Statement from 1 January to 31 October

Budget items	Annual budget 12 months	Budget Jan-Oct	Actual Jan-Oct	Difference Jan-Oct	% difference Jan-Oct	Notes
INCOME						
Department of Agriculture	200,000	200,000	200,000	0	0	
NGO grant	600,000	500,000	450,000	(50,000)	(10)	1
Miscellaneous income	110,000	91,700	93,400	1,700	2	
Fees and charges	2,600,000	2,350,000	1,655,000	(695,000)	(30)	2
Total income	**3,510,000**	**3,141,700**	**2,398,400**	**(743,300)**	**(24)**	
EXPENDITURE						
Purchases of supplies	1,200,000	1,050,000	940,600	109,400	10	3
Salaries	793,000	665,400	654,800	10,600	2	4
Rent	1,200,000	1,000,000	1,000,000	0	0	
Vehicle/other expenses	105,000	87,500	98,200	(10,700)	(12)	5
Equipment	200,000	200,000	205,000	(5,000)	(3)	
Loan/overdraft charge	12,000	10,000	8,500	1,500	15	6
Total expenditure	**3,510,000**	**3,012,900**	**2,907,100**	**105,800**	**4**	
Total income less total expenditure	0	128,800	(508,700)	(637,500)		

( ) Shows more budget than actual for 'income' items, and more actual than budget for 'expenditure' .

Notes
1. Grant from NGO has not yet been paid. Should be received in November.
2. Market price of supplies temporarily fell, and so charges were reduced from August onwards.
3. Cost of purchases was less because of fall in market prices. Some supplies were bought in advance.
4. One member of staff left in September and will not be replaced until November.
5. Vehicle needed major repairs in March. Telephone charges increased and are not included in the budget.
6. Balance of loan interest will be paid in December.

What can a 'budget and actual statement' tell us?

The statement in Table 1 shows the different items in the budget listed under 'income' and 'expenditure' in the left-hand column. The next column shows the funds allocated to each item. The 'budget' items are then compared with 'actual' income and expenditure for January to October. The next column shows the difference between them. The % column shows any major differences, and the notes explain why items are under or over the budgeted amount. In this example, the management committee or a manager might ask:

- Why has the NGO grant not been received, and does this have an impact (note 1)?
- Are the NGO and Department of Agriculture grants restricted to particular budget items?
- What is the longer-term impact of the fall in market prices (note 3)?
- How much of the supplies have been bought in advance (note 3)?
- What expenditure could we reduce in order to stay within the actual income?
- Who will fund the telephone costs not included in the budget (note 5)?
- Who will pay the 5,000 for equipment bought but not budgeted for?
- How much money is in our bank account – can we keep going?

Story: Budget and actual report

A Gender and Poverty project is funded by an Australian donor and has run for three years. The accountant and the co-ordinator worked together to ensure that the 'restricted' funding was fully utilised before the end of the funding period. They produced a monthly report to monitor spending against the approved budget.

One particular item was the stationery budget, which was set aside for workshop materials and looked as if it was going to be under-spent. To avoid returning the money, the project decided (with the approval of the donor) to buy the stationery for the partners who were working on the project and to distribute it to them so that they could use these materials in future workshop activities. The restricted funding budget was all utilised without having to return the balance to the donor, thanks to the information highlighted in the budget report.

(Oxfam, South Africa)

Cash-flow forecasting

In addition to the budget (which tells you if there is enough income to cover overall expenditure over the next year) and the monitoring report (which tells you how well or badly you are doing so far), a cash-flow forecast may also be useful. This tells you if you will have enough money to pay the bills as they fall due.

Story: Cash flow

An agricultural organisation had prepared a budget for the following year, assuming enough total income to cover all their expected expenditure. A major international donor had offered to contribute a large proportion of their funding, which they were keen to receive. But they knew that they would receive the income in two parts – the second part not until after the end of the budget year, even though they would have to pay for salaries, rent, and materials earlier. Staff thought that this would not be a problem.

One of their community groups suggested that they should examine their expected cash flow. This would help them to see when money would come in and go out, and when there might be shortages. They prepared a cash-flow forecast and found to their surprise that they had only enough money to cover expenditure for the next four months. After that, there would be three months when there would be no money at all, until the remaining funds arrived.

They approached the bank to ask for an overdraft. The bank refused, because they were a new organisation. They then talked to their donor, to ask if they could have the funds earlier. After careful negotiation, the donor agreed to pay the second part slightly earlier. They also delayed paying two months' salaries, and did some local fundraising.

When planning for future years, the management committee requested a cash-flow forecast, together with each annual budget. They also decided to talk to their donors about their policies of not paying the second instalment of grants until the work was completed. One donor could not agree, and so the organisation decided not to accept their funding again.

(From a training workshop, Serbia)

An administrator or finance person usually prepares the cash-flow forecast for the next six to twelve months. An example is shown in Table 2. A spreadsheet template, already programmed for preparing the cash-flow forecast and instructions on how to complete it, is freely available at www.johncammack.net (click on 'Resources').

Table 2: Example of a cash-flow forecast

Cash-Flow Forecast for the Southern Farmers' Support Organisation for the Six Months 1 January to 30 June

PERIOD	Jan	Feb	Mar	Apr	May	Jun
Money coming in						
Department of Agriculture	-	-	-	50,000	-	-
NGO grant	50,000	50,000	50,000	50,000	50,000	50,000
Miscellaneous income	9,000	5,000	9,000	9,000	10,000	10,000
Fees and charges	100,000	200,000	200,000	100,000	100,000	200,000
Total money coming in (B)	**159,000**	**255,000**	**259,000**	**209,000**	**160,000**	**260,000**
Money going out						
Purchases of supplies	80,000	80,000	120,000	120,000	100,000	150,000
Salaries	50,000	50,000	50,000	50,000	50,000	80,000
Rent	10,000	10,000	10,000	10,000	10,000	10,000
Vehicle/other expenses	12,000	12,000	12,000	3,000	2,000	5,000
Equipment	100,000	-	100,000	-	-	-
Loan/overdraft charge	-	-	-	-	-	3,500
Total money going out (C)	**252,000**	**152,000**	**292,000**	**183,000**	**162,000**	**248,500**
Summary						
Opening balance **(A)**	22,000	(71,000)	32,000	(1,000)	25,000	23,000
***Plus* total money coming in (B)**	159,000	255,000	259,000	209,000	160,000	260,000
***Less* total money going out (C)**	252,000	152,000	292,000	183,000	162,000	248,500
EXPECTED CLOSING BALANCE (A+B-C)	**(71,000)**	**32,000**	**(1,000)**	**25,000**	**23,000**	**34,500**

( ) on 'opening balance' and 'expected closing balance' figures shows that this is a shortage of money in cash and at the bank.

What can a 'cash-flow forecast' tell us?

The cash-flow forecast shows the money coming in and money going out over a future period. The 'expected closing balance' line tells us whether we have enough money for a particular month. A negative figure shows that we must arrange to pay 'money going out' items later, or receive 'money coming in' earlier. If this is not possible, a bank overdraft or temporary loan will be needed to keep the organisation going. In the example shown in Table 2, the management committee or manager might ask:

- How up to date is the forecast?
- How will the negative balances be covered in January and March?
- Will the Department of Agriculture or the NGO donor give us their money earlier?
- Can we delay paying any of the money going out?
- What does the forecast for the rest of the year show?
- If we compare this forecast with the budget and actual statement in Table 1, we can see that all the expected fees and charges were not received, and some of the expenditure has been under-spent or over-spent. How will the cash flow be affected by these factors?

The three documents together – budget, budget and actual statement, and the cash-flow forecast – give the management committee, the leader, managers, and anyone else who needs it a clear picture of how financially sound the organisation is.

Who needs to build budgeting capacity?

There are three main groups of people who need good budgeting skills.

The management committee

Members are responsible for the organisation's finances. They should approve the annual budget and annual financial statements and regularly compare actual income and expenditure with budgeted figures.

Ideally, one member of the management committee should have some experience of financial work and take a lead on budgeting issues. Other members should have enough understanding of budget information to be able to ask questions.

If members do not understand financial information, it is important to arrange appropriate training in how to interpret it, and the kinds of question to raise. Training could take place during one of their meetings. It might be provided by a member, or someone from another organisation, or a donor. Sometimes donors are happy to provide and/or fund this type of training.

If none of the members has any knowledge of finance, it is worth thinking about changing the membership. The next time you appoint new members, make sure that finances are treated as a high priority and the necessary skills needed are brought into the management committee. The committee will of course need many other skills too: in human resources, legal matters, gender equality, and social diversity.

Information received

Sometimes members do not take finance seriously because they cannot understand the information they have been given. They might receive pages of figures which are difficult to absorb, especially if not seen before the meeting. Box 1 gives guidance for presenting budgeting statements to meetings. The management committee should ask their finance people to follow these guidelines.

Box 1: How to present budgeting statements to committee meetings

- Identify why the information is needed: for example, to take decisions.
- Summarise the information; don't give all the details.
- Provide the budget and actual statement and details of your cash and bank position (or a cash-flow forecast) at least every three months.
- Make sure that the information is up to date and accurate.
- Use no more than one side of paper when presenting the information.
- Think about using visual presentations instead of numbers: for example, pie charts.
- Circulate information to members before the meeting.
- When talking at the meeting, select a few key figures.
- Be brief – a few minutes should be enough.
- Make it easy for people to discuss and ask questions; encourage people to ask for more detailed information if they need it.

Leaders and managers

For organisations that employ paid staff, much of what has been said in the section above about management committees also applies to leaders and managers. They should prepare and monitor the budget for their work area and take any necessary action when they are presented with a budget and actual statement. Often this information will be prepared by an administrator or finance person. The budget and actual statement may be the same outline information as presented to the management committee, but with more detail.

Leaders and managers do not always have the special skills needed to manage budgets. In such a case, they will need training to understand the format and content of a budget. Sometimes an 'umbrella group' or donor might provide this kind of training for community-based organisations and non-government organisations.

The leadership team should feel a sense of 'ownership' of the budget. The budget should not be seen as belonging exclusively to the finance people, just because they produced it. The more the leadership and managers are involved in, and trusted with, the design of reports, the more they will value them.

Finance people

Finance people often produce budget and actual statements in a format designed for their own purposes, rather than for the management committee, the leader, or managers. If, for example, a standard computerised accounting package is used, it may not produce the budget and actual statement in a way that is helpful for the organisation. It is important that finance people understand the reasons why information is required. Box 2 shows how this information can be identified and produced.

Box 2: How to improve the presentation of budgeting information

Ask ...

- the management committee and managers what level of budget and actual statements they need – summarised or detailed – and involve them in the design;
- the management committee why they need the information, for example to help to take a specific decision;
- other organisations about the way in which they present information.

Then ...

- If the budget and actual statement is prepared manually, prepare the different versions as requested.
- If working with a computerised accounting package, explore the possibilities of producing the information in different versions.
- Try downloading (or if necessary re-inputting) the information into a computer spreadsheet programme and adapting the information to the format that you want.
- In the longer term, if you are computerised, give non-finance people access to a 'read-only' version of financial data.

Finance staff do not need to be highly qualified in order to prepare budget and actual statements in different formats. Less experienced staff, however, may not know the possibilities available, so a member of the leadership team may need to take the initiative. Sometimes external auditors or donors will make suggestions.

As organisations grow, the information previously available is no longer sufficient to meet their needs. They can either try to manage with poor-quality reports, or they can invest in improvements. For organisations working with a paper-based system, this might involve training staff to present information in more easily understood formats. For organisations with computers, hardware and software may need upgrading and staff may need to be trained in the new systems. Changing software can be a big task, but may produce much better information with less staff effort. Donors can sometimes help to fund the changes (see 'Financial information' in Chapter 8). If you are considering a change, you should seek advice from a qualified accountant or auditor.

Box 3: Planning and budgeting – common concerns	
Concerns	**Possible solutions**
Our budgets are not prepared and approved before the start of the programme activity or financial year.	Encourage advance planning in order to set objectives for the next year. Tie the budget to the planning process and fix the meeting dates of the management committee. Make these dates known and ask for progress reports at each meeting. Arrange for the management committee meeting to approve the final budget several weeks before the start of the year.

Box continues overleaf

Concerns	Possible solutions
All the budgetary decisions are taken by one person, usually our finance person.	Start the next budget cycle by arranging a meeting for those responsible for activities to talk about objectives and priorities. Convince this group that these can only be achieved if they take part in the budget process. If necessary, involve finance people or an external facilitator to offer training in preparing budgets. Have clear timetables, with budget formats prepared in advance.
Our budget does not fully represent our organisation's values on matters such as gender and diversity.	Make sure that all appropriate voices are heard at the budget-planning stage. Finance staff may need training in 'gender budgeting' issues (see 'Websites' at the end of this book).
The objectives agreed in our original plan for this year are not fully reflected in the budget.	If you discover this before the budget is approved by the management committee and funding has been agreed, add the missing items, and make sure that all other objectives are included. If you discover it after approval, assess how vital they are this year, and talk to your donor to see if you can get additional funding. If successful, ask the management committee to approve it, adding these items.
Our budget and actual statements are always produced two/three months after the period has ended.	Talk to the finance people and ask why there is a delay and what can be done to avoid it. It may be that the statements are not prioritised (because people don't use them), or there may be resource-related problems: for example not enough staff, or outdated software.

Concerns	Possible solutions
No budget monitoring takes place.	Make sure that the management committee have budget monitoring on the agenda for each meeting. Produce a simple monitoring report monthly/quarterly for these meetings. Ask managers to use this too.
Our management committee show no interest in financial information.	Make sure that the information is designed for the right audience. Don't assume that one size fits all. A finance person on the management committee may raise the profile of finance.
Managers and the management committee members do not understand what is presented.	Organise training to help them to interpret the reports. If possible, ask finance people to do this, or invite an outside facilitator to attend one of the regular meetings.
Regular items such as electricity and telephone charges are only charged once or twice a year.	Include an estimate of these items each time a report is produced, so that it gives a truer picture. Ask finance people how they can help with this.
Staff who overspend their budgets are not asked to explain why.	Persuade the leadership team of the importance of this matter. Staff responsible for budgets should meet with their managers to explain any over-spending.
Income promised has not been received. We may not continue.	Act immediately. Warn the management committee. Contact donors. Prepare a cash-flow forecast to see how long you have money to carry on. Spend on essential items only.

4 | Accounts record-keeping

This chapter looks at the records kept and some monthly routines completed in medium-sized organisations. It also suggests matters that a leader or manager might follow up when reviewing the monthly accounts.

What would you expect to see?

The accounting system is likely to be based on one of the following:

- a paper-based system
- a paper-based system supported by computer spreadsheets
- an 'off the shelf' computerised accounting package
- (for large organisations) a specially designed accounting package.

The following records are often kept, whatever system is in place:

- **Cash/bank book**, for each currency. This gives a daily listing for money coming in and money going out, for cash and bank separately.
- **Bank records** (bank statement or bank pass book).
- A record agreeing differences between the bank statement/pass book with your bank book, called a '**bank reconciliation**'.
- **Payroll details.**
- **Cash advances and loans registers.** These show details of sums advanced, repaid, accounted for, and still outstanding.
- **Records of funds given for a particular purpose**, what has been spent, and how much is left.
- **Invoices and receipts** that explain expenditure in the cash/bank book.
- Details of money owing to you (called '**debtors**' or '**receivables**') and what you owe to others (called '**creditors**' or '**payables**').

All computerised accounting systems must have paper-based information to back up the electronic information. Auditors always examine the paper records as well as computerised records. Larger organisations with more complex accounting requirements need additional records, for example:

- **A ledger.** This shows expenditure by type. Computerised accounting packages are based on the ledger.

- **A journal.** This records adjustments in the accounts, for example because of errors. It is part of the ledger system of accounting.

These two documents need to be kept by a trained book-keeper. Organisations using them are also likely to have a computerised accounting package, and will produce an income and expenditure account and a balance sheet at the end of the year.

Monthly routines

Introducing monthly routines helps to ensure that the accounting record-keeping capacity covers everything that the organisation needs. A finance person completes these routines, but the leader/manager then checks them, signs them off, and takes any further action that is necessary. The actual routines will depend on the size and complexity of the organisation, and might include those shown in Box 4.

Box 4: Example of monthly accounting routines	
Monthly routine	**Possible further action by leader/manager**
Update the cash/bank book.	Check that all transactions have supporting documents (for example, invoices or receipts).
	Count the cash and check that it agrees with the cash balance in the cash/bank book.
Agree the cash/bank book (your record) with each bank statement (the process known as a 'bank reconciliation').	Make sure you see the bank statement; check that the two records agree, and that the reasons for any differences are appropriate.
	Follow up any cause for concern.

Box continues overleaf

Monthly routine	Possible further action by leader/manager
Update details of cash advances and loans to staff. (Cash advances and loans registers may be used.)	Talk to anyone with a cash advance outstanding for more than a month.
List members of staff to be paid.	Approve payroll for payment. Make sure you know all the staff listed.
List organisations that owe you money and those that you owe money to.	Contact those who owe you money that have not paid for more than a month. Initial contact should be by mail/email; after two months, by telephone or personal visit.
Compare actual income and expenditure with the budget from start of the year to date.	Focus on large differences and take any necessary action.
List income/expenditure committed but not yet received/paid.	Check if the commitments change any of the 'actual' figures in the budget and actual statement. If any donor funds have not been received, contact the donor.
Calculate current cash-flow position.	Identify any shortages over the next few months and decide what to do.
Update stock records (if used).	Check stock records and make random checks at the warehouse on individual items. Check all the stock several times a year.
List any donor reporting needed over the next three months.	Make sure the information will be built into work plans and available on time.

Box 5: Accounts record-keeping – common concerns

Concerns	Possible solutions
Invoices and receipts are not always available to back up our transactions.	Insist on receiving the correct paperwork before making any payment. Have separate files for 'money coming in' and 'money going out'.
Cash advances to our staff are not recorded and are out of control.	Start a cash-advances register to show amounts advanced, repaid, or accounted for, and what is outstanding. A senior person should review this each month and speak to those with unaccounted for advances.
Our accounts do not show whether 'restricted' funds have been used for the purpose given.	If you use a paper-based system, start a new book to record restricted funds, and make sure this is linked to expenditure. A computerised accounting system may have a facility for allocating the expenditure to a particular donor.
No one knows what money is due to be received.	A separate record of amounts due (sometimes called 'debtors' or 'receivables') will record any funding promised or invoices sent out. Keep a file divided into two halves; at the front, file details of money that should be received. When it is received, write the date, amount received, and reference; move this information to the back of the file. Review outstanding amounts each month and follow them up if necessary.

Box continues overleaf

Concerns	Possible solutions
Staff do not know how our organisation wants them to claim expenses, approve expenditure, and take advances.	If there is a written policy, see if it is understandable. If it is, circulate it. If not, consider writing down clearly how things should be done. In the longer term, putting things in writing is good practice for all financial tasks. Arrange some basic training on this procedure for existing staff, and make it part of the induction programme for new staff.
Only one person in our office can answer questions about invoices due to be paid.	More than one person needs to understand the records well enough to answer questions and take action, if the finance person is not in the office. Look at the jobs and find tasks that someone else can do regularly, so they too become familiar with the records in future. In a small organisation the leader (or in a large organisation the manager) should also be able to do this.
Our finance person is the only person who looks at the accounting records.	Introduce a system where the leader or manager sees the accounting records monthly. These should include at least the cash/bank book with invoices/receipts, the bank statement and reconciliation, and the advances/loans register. In larger organisations other records will be added. At the same time, count and agree any cash balance (this should also be counted and agreed weekly). The leader/ manager should sign the records to confirm approval. If only one person sees the accounts, there is a danger of theft.

5 | Financial reporting

In this chapter we consider the different types of financial report needed for stakeholders. They include the annual accounting statements, which are often a legal requirement.

The 'budget and actual' report (shown in Chapter 3) is produced for the leadership team and managers. Organisations may also need the following financial reports for their external stakeholders:

- annual accounting statements
- reports to donors (and 'narrative' reports on the programme activities)
- reports to government (for example, concerning tax or foreign contributions)
- reports to beneficiaries, communities, and partner groups

Each of these reports offers challenges to finance staff. Ideally the financial information is kept in a system that is flexible enough to present reports in different formats when needed, to suit internal and external users. Some computerised accounting packages can do this, but many organisations only use computer spreadsheets, or they have to produce these reports manually.

Annual accounting statements

Most organisations, even small ones, produce a statement at the end of their financial year, to report what they have done with the funds given to them. These are presented in two main ways:

Receipts and payments account

The receipts and payments account (sometimes called a 'cash account') shows a summary of all cash and bank money coming in (receipts) and going out (payments) over the last year. It is the simplest form of accounting statement. Items bought for longer-term use, for example vehicles or computers, are listed alongside the day-to-day items such as rent and salaries.

All the information for a receipts and payments account comes from the organisation's own records. It shows:

- the amount held in cash and bank at the beginning of the year
- plus money received (receipts)
- less money paid (payments)
- the amount held in cash and bank at the end of the year.

It does not show whether a surplus or a deficit has been made, only what money is left. The receipts and payments account is usually produced by small groups with a single purpose or activity and few staff. Its main advantage is that it can be prepared by someone who has not been trained in technical accounting.

Income and expenditure account

The income and expenditure account (sometimes called *account of operations, income statement, income and disbursement account, operating statement, statement of earnings,* or *statement of financial activities*) is an annual accounting statement to show what has happened over the last year. It shows the cash and bank amounts, but also additional items. For example, an amount due for payment in the year (for example the outstanding end-of-year telephone charge) will be included, even though it has not yet been paid. This means that the account shows a full 12 months' income and expenditure, and can be compared with the budget and previous year's accounting statements. Ideally the account should also show 'restricted' and 'unrestricted' funds separately (see Chapter 10, Box 17).

The income and expenditure account is usually presented with a *balance sheet.* A balance sheet shows what the organisation owns (buildings, vehicles, equipment, and the amount in the bank account); what it owes (outstanding payments to suppliers and loans); and where the money has come from to fund what it owns (usually money built up from surpluses in previous years and any unspent donor funds held). These items are not included in the income and expenditure account.

The income and expenditure account and the balance sheet, and the records that support them, are more technical than the receipts and payments account. To prepare them you will need to employ a trained book-keeper, or ask an accountant or an accounting firm to help you.

A full explanation of these annual accounting statements is outside the scope of this book. Useful publications are listed in the 'Further reading' list at the back of this book.

Financial and management accounting

Some accounting is usually required by national law, which differs from country to country. The management committee and finance person must be aware of the appropriate requirements and they must keep records from the very beginning of the organisation's activities. This information, called 'financial accounting', does not always provide all that is required for managing an organisation and informing decisions.

Box 6: Differences between financial and management accounting	
Financial accounting	**Management accounting**
Examples include annual accounting statements (for example, the income and expenditure account and balance sheet).	Examples include the budget and the 'budget and actual' statement.
Required by law.	Leaders and managers decide to produce it.
Shown to all stakeholders/donors.	Only used internally, but donors may see it.
Is usually audited.	Does not have to be audited.
Layout follows a standard format.	Layout designed to help users to take decisions.

Budgeting reports, for example, are produced for internal use, and usually there is no legal requirement, although donors often insist on a budget being produced. Budget information is part of 'management accounting'.

At some point in an organisation's growth, more 'management accounting' information will be needed to help it to manage its activities more effectively. This may result in some extra financial work, although most computerised accounting packages can produce information in financial and management accounting formats. Sometimes a 'management accountant' is appointed specifically to develop these reports.

Financial reports to donors

Donors usually ask for reports on the use of the funds that they have given, often presented in their own format. These may include the following:

- A budget and actual statement, every quarter and at the end of their financial year, with notes to explain any changes (see Chapter 3).
- The audited annual accounting statements, for example the receipts and payments account or income and expenditure account and balance sheet.
- A separate report listing income and expenditure for parts of the programme that the donor has funded.
- Copies of (or original) invoices.

Reporting back to donors

It is essential to send reports to the donor by the agreed date. Include these reports in work plans, to make sure that deadlines are not missed. Also:

- Make sure that there is consistency between the donor's budget format and the budget format that you use in your accounting system. If your system cannot produce information in the donor's format, negotiate with the donor to accept your format, or think about ways of satisfying the donor but avoiding additional work. This makes reporting easier and maintains good relations with the donor.
- Think about whether the level of your accounting skills is sufficient. A large amount of new donor funding will increase your income and activities – and the systems required to support them. Make sure you have the appropriate capacity to manage and account for new programmes before accepting the funding. This includes the financial capacity at all the sites where you operate.

Financial reports to government

Some governments will want full reports on everything you do, including:

- staff tax deducted from salary
- organisational tax
- amounts paid to staff
- contributions from international organisations.

Reports to beneficiaries

It is important to report to your beneficiaries, communities, and partner groups. 'External relationships' in Chapter 8 offers suggestions on how to do this.

Donors and government often ask for reports to be presented in their own formats. These may be different from your own. Try to minimise the work required for reports to your existing or potential stakeholders. Ask someone to give you advice on how to make your accounting system more efficient, so that it can provide reports in a range of formats.

Box 7: Financial reporting – common concerns	
Concerns	**Possible solutions**
Our accounting statements are only produced ten months after the year-end.	Find out why they are late, and if there is anything you can do to produce them earlier. The delay may be due to your staff, or the auditors. Out-of-date statements are not so useful as current statements. Statements should be produced no later than six months after the year-end.
The management committee do not approve our end-of-year accounting statements.	Arrange the timing of their meeting to coincide with the production of the statements. Put the need for approval on the agenda, and circulate the accounts to members in advance.
Our computerised accounting package will not automatically produce the reports that we require for donors.	Talk to donors and ask if they are willing to accept what you already produce. If not, talk with someone who knows about the accounting system, and see if they can advise you. Think about buying or creating a system that will do what you want.

Box continues overleaf

Concerns	Possible solutions
The government wants us to produce a statement in a different format from the one we use.	This may mean producing two statements each year. If you have a paper-based accounting system, this may involve considerably more work. If you have a computerised accounting system, investigate whether it can produce both formats from the accounting records. Could the information be downloaded to a computer spreadsheet which could then be amended?
We do not have a computerised accounting system, and preparing reports for different stakeholders takes too much time.	It may be possible to computerise your accounting to reduce the time taken, but don't rush it. Talk with your donors to see if they can fund the computer hardware and software, and training for staff.
Only the finance person prepares and reviews financial reports before they are sent to donors.	Financial reports need to be consistent with other reports about the programme. Someone other than the people preparing reports should review them, to ensure that they are consistent.
We do not understand national financial reporting guidelines and so we do not always follow them.	Get a copy of the guidelines (if available). Ask for advice from other organisations or a professional accountant in your country.

6 | Financial controls

This chapter considers financial controls and best practice in using them. It also looks at what happens if things go wrong, and how these risks can be minimised.

Financial (or internal) controls are essential for any group or organisation. They help an organisation to prevent errors and the possibility of theft. Most importantly, financial controls help to protect reputations.

The leadership team and managers are responsible for making sure that there are good financial controls in place, and in some countries the management committee is legally responsible for this. If appointed, professional accounting staff (or external auditors) can advise on what systems are needed and how to introduce them.

What are financial controls?

Financial controls are the financial and management systems that aim to protect an organisation's property and minimise the risk of error and theft.

Is trust enough?

In the non-profit sector, people sometimes say that controls are not necessary, as everyone trusts each other. Although trust is important, controls are needed in order to prove to stakeholders and others outside the organisation that the leadership team are making effective use of money donated by individuals or organisations.

Story: Financial controls

CAMFED Zimbabwe, established in 1993, is dedicated to fighting poverty and HIV and AIDS in rural communities by educating girls.

The communities where CAMFED works had little experience of financial controls, so the organisation offered training to help people to put controls in place. CAMFED has a culture of trust and respect in these communities, and financial controls are a central part of this relationship.

The controls are there to protect everybody: the organisation from theft or poor planning; volunteers and staff from false allegations or misunderstandings; and the beneficiaries themselves – as every dollar helps to improve the girls' education.

Introducing controls does not hinder CAMFED's work in the communities, but rather helps it to build on the trust that has already been built up. Controls have helped CAMFED to:

- understand its own organisation better and take better decisions
- strengthen its relationship with the Ministry of Education
- attract more donations in cash and 'in-kind'
- show people where the money is spent, and therefore increase their commitment to the task of educating girls.

(CAMFED Zimbabwe)

The key financial controls include the following:

- **Cash controls**: systems for managing cash amounts.
- **Bank controls**: systems for making sure that the bank account cannot be misused.
- **Budgeting and accounting controls**: systems that provide sufficient information to manage the activities of the organisation.
- **Purchase and authorisation controls**: making sure that different people are involved at each stage.
- **Management controls**: extra checks made by management.
- **Physical controls**: keeping property and equipment in good order and secure; and guidance on the personal use of items owned by the organisation.

Developing good financial controls is central to building financial management capacity. To identify weaknesses in your organisation, use the Review of Financial Systems in Appendix B. Examples of best practice are listed below.

Best practice: 'top 10' principles for controlling cash

- Keep the minimum amount of cash needed for you to operate efficiently.
- Record all cash items received or paid in a cash book as soon as possible after the transaction has taken place.
- Issue pre-printed numbered receipts, with the organisation's name, for any cash received, and keep a copy.
- Request a receipt and keep it when money is paid out in cash.
- Keep cash in a secure place – preferably in a lockable tin which is kept in a safe. If not, use a locked cupboard or drawer.
- A senior person should count the cash regularly and check that it agrees with the cash book. This person and the cashier should sign the cash book to confirm that the count has been made.
- Someone other than the cashier should authorise any large or unusual payments. Set a limit above which the cashier must obtain the approval of a manager.
- The person responsible for cash (the 'cashier') should not (ideally) be the one dealing with other accounting records.
- The cashier should check regularly how much cash is left and tell a senior person if there is not enough for day-to-day operations.
- Make one person responsible for the control of cash at any one time. When a new person takes over, both people should agree and sign the cash balance.

Best practice: 'top 10' principles for controlling bank accounts

- Register bank accounts in the name of a group or organisation – never in the name of an individual.
- Tell the bank that all requests for withdrawals (cheques, for example) should be signed by two people. Sometimes it is more practical to require 'any two signatories from three named individuals'.
- Never sign blank cheques, or expect others to do so.
- Each time that the bank statement is received (or the pass book is updated), check that the organisation's own bank records in the cash/bank book agree with it.
- Write cheques for as many payments as possible, to avoid holding large amounts of cash.
- Transfer large amounts directly through the bank from one account to another.
- Pay money into the bank as often as practical, to avoid keeping large sums of cash on the premises. In rural locations, this cannot be done very often. Make use of people going to the town where the bank is, to pay money in. Cheques can sometimes be requested to avoid large amounts of cash building up. If cash is held, it must be kept securely.
- The person who is involved in the preparation of cheques should not also sign them.
- Keep cheque books in a safe, locked cupboard or drawer.
- Keep the fewest possible separate bank accounts, although some donors will insist that you keep a separate bank account for their funds.

Best practice: 'top 10' principles for budgeting and accounting controls

- Prepare the budget in line with organisational objectives before the start of the year, and get the management committee to approve it.
- Produce the budget and actual reports as soon as possible after the end of the period.
- Add notes to explain large differences in the budget and actual statement.
- Compare regular summaries of income and expenditure with the budget. Make sure that the management committee and managers monitor the summaries.
- Prepare a cash-flow forecast to show when shortages may occur.
- Record everything, keeping accurate and up-to-date accounting records.
- Make sure that there is a supporting document (an invoice, for example) for every transaction, and file the documents in order.
- Keep a system to alert you when money is still owed to you.
- Record 'restricted' donor funding separately in the accounting system.
- Provide financial reports when required and include them in work plans.

Best practice: 'top 10' principles for purchase and authorisation controls

- Make sure there is a budget for goods and services ordered.
- Allow only nominated people to place orders.
- Ask for at least three quotes for goods and services valued at more than a certain amount.
- Check goods and services received for quality before paying for them.
- Match invoices against original orders, and pay on original invoices only.
- Keep clear records of money owing and paid to other people.
- Do regular stock-takes of goods held, and check that they agree with stock records.
- A senior person should authorise expenditure before it is made.
- Cheques should be authorised by a different person from the one who signs them.
- Ask self-employed individuals to provide evidence of their self-employed status before making a payment (so that if you don't deduct tax, you are not liable to pay it to the tax authorities).

Best practice: 'top 10' principles for management controls

- Allocate responsibilities to staff.
- Write job descriptions for staff and volunteers.
- Recruit suitably qualified staff and volunteers: check their references and qualifications.
- Identify and deal with staff who are not performing adequately.
- Make sure that everyone knows the policies and procedures. Write them down and talk about them regularly, for example in staff meetings.
- Develop staff and volunteers, for example through induction and training for new staff.
- Arrange an annual external audit.
- Act on the auditor's recommendations.
- Write minutes for all meetings.
- Communicate openly with staff, volunteers, and other stakeholders.

Best practice: 'top 10' principles for physical controls

- Keep all premises locked and safe.
- Allow only authorised staff and volunteers to use premises and equipment.
- Keep an up-to-date record of items owned, and check it regularly.
- Register all items in the organisation's name.
- Keep stock records for purchases, items issued, and the balance left.
- Count stock regularly and agree it with the records.
- Arrange insurance cover, if possible, for valuable items, including cash.
- Write clear policies on the use of equipment: for example, vehicles and photocopiers.
- Keep confidential information locked away.
- Use a safe for cash, cheque books, and other valuable documents.

When things go wrong

Non-profit organisations are often very trusting of their staff, but they need to recognise that theft, or 'fraud', can and does happen. Some of the most vulnerable organisations are those that prefer not to think about the possibility of fraud and therefore ignore it.

> **What is fraud?**
>
> Using deception to obtain an organisation's money, goods, or services for personal gain.

Examples of fraud include altering or forging cheques, making out cheques for personal payments, claiming for travel expenses not incurred, and theft of cash, stock, or equipment. Often records are altered to try to cover up the fraud. Errors or mistakes are not fraud but, if not detected, can lead to fraud, for example by giving a staff member an opportunity to hide things and exploit the error.

The damage done by fraud can be calculated in terms of the amount stolen, but the biggest damage is to the organisation's reputation. There is also a hidden cost of staff time and morale in creating new systems and repairing the reputation of the organisation. Prepare your organisation as if fraud is going to happen.

Knowing when things are going wrong

Although it is impossible to detect all frauds, tight financial controls will help to alert you when things are not right. There are a number of other accounting signs or clues to look out for:

- accounting records are inaccurate, corrected, and/or out of date;
- bank statements and 'bank reconciliations' are missing;
- invoices, receipts, bank statements, and other documents are often missing;
- financial and stock records contain many errors.

These are not necessarily fraud, but you should be suspicious.

Use regular budget monitoring reports to track whether the figures follow the expected pattern. Ask questions if, for example, the start of a project has been delayed, but its telephone and travel costs are still being paid.

Notice if people behave differently. If someone is suddenly buying lots of expensive items, think about where they might have obtained the money. Although there may be innocent explanations, if people are working long hours, not leaving their desks, not taking holidays, or are very tired and making mistakes, this could mean that they are covering up a fraud. Frauds are sometimes discovered when people are away sick. When you suspect something, this is an opportunity for you to investigate what is going on.

Story: Weak financial controls

The organisation had grown from a small group of volunteers. It now had paid staff, its own premises, and a range of programme activities. It had always believed that it had good financial controls.

One day its bank telephoned to ask if the organisation had written a cash cheque recently for €5,000 from its foreign-currency account. The signature on the cheque was OK, but the bank had noticed that it came from a separate sequence of numbered cheques.

The accountant knew immediately that she had not written it. The cheque was from a cheque book that had not been used and was kept in a locked cupboard. She only used foreign-currency cheques occasionally, so she would not have noticed this missing cheque for some time. Unfortunately the cheque had been accompanied by a letter of authority on headed notepaper, which the bank had taken as genuine and so had cashed the cheque a few days earlier.

On investigating the name of the person cashing the cheque, the accountant discovered that he had visited the organisation some months before. She could only assume that he had been left in the office alone, the cupboard was left unlocked, and he had stolen the cheque and the headed notepaper. He then forged the cheque signatures from a cheque that had actually been issued to him. The man was eventually arrested and sent to prison, although the €5,000 was never found.

(From a training workshop, Germany)

Steps to minimise fraud

Introduce 'separation of duties'

Separation of duties affects every area of financial control. It aims to prevent errors and theft by making sure that one person is not responsible for the whole of any transaction, for example placing an order, authorising a payment, and signing a cheque. There should be a different person to carry out each task.

Small organisations do not always have enough staff for work to be separated. They should involve someone else on an occasional basis, for example counting cash when an outside member of staff visits, or asking a local firm of accountants to make surprise checks. Being a small organisation is not an excuse for poor financial controls. It is a reason to think carefully about ways to introduce them. You may need to ask a qualified accountant for more advice.

Make sure there are good financial controls

- The leader and senior staff should publicly make it very clear that theft of any sort is totally unacceptable.
- Explain to staff that controls are important for the protection of the organisation and staff, even if sometimes hard to follow.
- Senior staff themselves should follow the rules strictly.
- The leadership team should implement controls and be prepared for possible fraud.
- Accurate and up-to-date financial information should be available in a user-friendly format.
- Leaders and managers should sign off monthly accounts and make random checks on financial systems.
- Leaders and managers should follow up any complaints received.
- When recruiting staff and volunteers, always follow up references and check certificates of qualifications.
- Provide training in financial management.
- Arrange a regular external audit.

Make it easy for staff to tell someone if they are suspicious

Create a culture that makes it easy for staff to share concerns – but this should be done responsibly and with specific evidence.

Introduce a confidential 'whistle-blowing' scheme, explaining what this is and the sorts of issue that might need reporting.

What is 'whistle-blowing'?

Providing staff and volunteers with a procedure for confidentially reporting a concern about the conduct of a colleague, for example if mishandling of money is suspected. This would usually be reported to their manager, but a nominated senior member of staff or member of the management committee should be an alternative. The organisation then has a duty to investigate the issue and take any necessary action.

Have a clearly defined policy to combat fraud

- Set up routine controls.
- Specify how people can report their concerns.
- Specify when to tell the police.
- Identify the person who is responsible for any investigation.
- Prescribe how an investigation can be conducted sensitively.
- Identify the documents that should be protected as evidence.
- Prescribe how to record all incidents in a fraud register (see below).

This fraud policy should be made known to all staff. It should be updated after any theft or fraud is suspected or proved.

How to survive and respond

The organisation needs to be able to learn from any incidents of theft or fraud. A key way to do this is through a 'fraud register'. This states the date and details of the incident, who was involved, the value of any lost property, a description of what happened, action taken, and lessons learned. You may need to check whether it is legal to keep anyone's name in such a register.

Make sure that any lessons learned are written down in full, and any necessary changes to the financial controls are made throughout the organisation.

This may be a stressful time, and it is very important that those involved receive support from colleagues and friends. Members of staff who are not directly involved may feel that they too are suspected, so you need to rebuild their trust. This can sometimes be achieved positively by involving staff in a discussion about the possible risks and what could be done to avoid something similar occurring.

Organisations are sometimes reluctant to tell their donors about an incident of fraud; but generally it is better that donors hear about it from you, rather than someone else.

Box 8: Financial controls – common concerns

Concerns	Possible solutions
Our organisation has grown recently, and our financial controls are inadequate.	Use the *Review of Financial Systems* in Appendix B. If you have an external auditor, ask him or her to help you.
Only the cashier counts the office cash.	Ask someone other than the cashier to count the cash, on a different day each week. Calculate the current balance from the cash book and confirm that it agrees with the cash available. If not, find out why. Reassure the cashier that this is best practice and that you don't suspect them of anything.
I suspect that someone is using the vehicle for private journeys.	Use a vehicle log-book to record all journeys, showing the destination, the milometer readings at the start and end of the journey, the day and time, and the reason for the journey. Check the log book against the vehicle reading.
Equipment in the office seems to be missing, but no one knows what should be there.	Write down a record of everything owned (an 'inventory') and keep it up to date. Check the items against it at least once a year.
Money that is owed to us is not received, and no one follows it up.	Issue invoices for goods or services promptly, and file a copy for reminders to be sent. Include a check on whether the debts are paid, and any follow-up, in the monthly accounting routines.
Our receipts are not pre-numbered.	Receipts could be issued for income and the money could be stolen, because there is no record of the missing receipt. Number all financial stationery so that it can be traced.

Box continues overleaf

Concerns	Possible solutions
We are a small organisation and know each other well. We don't bother about fraud.	Be aware of what could go wrong and build steps to minimise fraud. Organisations that ignore the possibility of fraud can be very vulnerable.
I am convinced that someone is stealing money, but there is no way of telling the organisation.	Talk with your manager, a senior staff member, or a member of the management committee. Introduce a formal procedure for staff in these situations (a 'whistle-blowing' policy), and tell everyone about it.
One of our staff who stole money has now been dismissed, and we need to learn lessons from this.	Review all the financial systems. Write down what has happened in a 'fraud register'. Support staff and others who have been affected. Ensure that controls are in place so that it cannot happen again.

7 | External audit

This chapter discusses how an external audit can help to build financial management capacity. It considers the appropriate levels of audit for organisations of various sizes, the services you can expect from an auditor, and what documentation to expect or ask for.

External audit is a valuable tool of capacity builders. At best, annual audits offer an opportunity for an independent review of an organisation's records and systems, with recommendations for improvements. Encouraging external audits and making sure that their recommendations are taken seriously will improve financial management capacity.

However, not all organisations will either have, or legally need, an audit. There are three categories of organisation:

- **small**, where either an external audit is not legally required or it has not been thought necessary;

- **small to medium-sized**, where a formal legal audit may not be required, but a less demanding inspection by an 'independent examiner' is done instead;

- **medium to large**, where an audit may be required by law and/or by donors.

It is important to check the legal requirements in the country in which you work. Even if it is not legally required, your organisation is likely to benefit from an audit.

Services you can expect from an auditor

An external auditor, from a firm of accountants, may offer different types of audit, some of which are described below.

Financial audits

A financial audit is an independent analysis of the accounting records and end-of-year accounting statements. At the end of this process, the auditor will give an 'opinion'.

What is an audit 'opinion'?

The auditor expresses an opinion at the end of the audit about whether the accounts give a 'true and fair view' of the organisation's activity. A positive (or 'unqualified') opinion is given in most audits. A negative (or 'qualified') opinion is less common, and a cause of concern for the organisation. It suggests that something is not right. The organisation's donors and other stakeholders will all see the opinion.

Management (or systems) audits

A management audit looks at the management and financial processes and systems. It examines how effective these are and makes recommendations for any necessary improvements.

Many audit firms will undertake both financial and management audits. The management audit, if well done, is more useful to help to build an organisation's financial and management capacity. You should agree in advance on the type of audit to be provided, and include it in the terms of reference or 'letter of engagement'. A management audit may include the following components:

- an assessment of financial and management systems; for example, examining if the authorisation system is adequate, rather than merely identifying whether a particular purchase had the proper authorisation;
- judging whether budgeting reports are in an understandable format;
- asking whether donor funding is meeting its objectives.

Not all external auditors would feel happy to assess particular aspects of a management audit; they may not even see it as their job. They will only do a financial audit.

If your auditor either does not do management audits or is unable to help you to build financial management capacity, you could use the information and questions in this book as a starting point. Ideally, it should be a joint effort between management and auditor, but management is ultimately responsible for building capacity. You might want to think about using an external facilitator, if your auditor is not able to help.

Other types of audit, for example examining the impact of an organisation's programme activities, are sometimes carried out only by larger audit firms.

Independent examination

An examination is less thorough than a full audit. It is done by someone who knows something about accounting but is not necessarily a qualified accountant. He or she may make the examination as a volunteer.

The process involves examining the accounting records and statements, but it is unlikely to cover a full management audit. It is suitable for small organisations. It will not usually provide an 'opinion' or written recommendations. The examination confirms the truthfulness of the accounts, but is less helpful for building financial management capacity.

Independent examination is known by different names. It is sometimes called 'an inspection', or simply 'an audit', because it is difficult to tell the difference.

External and internal audits

An external audit is carried out by a qualified accountant or auditor. This is often someone from an 'accounting firm' or 'accounting partnership', whose key quality is independence from the organisation that is being audited. When an employee of the organisation conducts a review of financial controls, systems, and processes, it is an internal audit. Internal audit is not often used in the non-profit sector, except in large organisations. However, donors will sometimes want their own auditors to examine an organisation's systems and records. This may be instead of, or in addition to, the annual external audit.

Using an audit to build capacity

Although independent examiners may not give written documents at the end of their inspection, if an external auditor is from an accounting firm, you can expect recommendations (sometimes called 'a management letter') and an audit report.

Recommendations

Towards the end of the audit, the auditor will raise concerns which have not been resolved, and will make recommendations for change. These will be shared in a draft letter written to the management committee or leader. The organisation clarifies and, if possible, answers the points made. Some items are then deleted from later versions of the letter. The final version of the letter may include comments by the management on the points raised. It will include recommendations and identify matters that need attention either immediately or, more usually, before the next annual audit. An example is shown in Box 9.

Box 9: Extract from a management letter

1. A number of advances to staff were outstanding and not fully accounted for at 31 December. A more comprehensive system of financial control is required to ensure that these are followed up.

Management comment on paragraph 1
These advances have subsequently been accounted for in full. A new advances register has been introduced, to ensure that no new advances will be issued until accounts are provided for any outstanding ones.

2. Payment vouchers and connected documents have not been stamped to state that they have been paid. All of these should be so stamped and dated, to avoid the possible reuse of a document.

Management comment on paragraph 2
The office has not held a 'paid' stamp. However, one has now been purchased and a system introduced to make sure that all documents are stamped.

3. Grant income received from international donors has not always been spent in the way specified by the donor. The Centre's accounting records do not show income which has been given for a particular purpose identified separately.

Management comment on paragraph 3
We accept the auditors' observation that the accounting records do not separately identify all income received for a particular purpose. A new accounting procedure has been introduced which will rectify this.

We do not, however, accept that grant income received was not used for the purpose given. We understood that this income was unrestricted and as such it was used towards the general running costs of the Centre.

Source: Financial Management for Development [4]

The management letter is a valuable contribution to the organisation's on-going development and capacity-building. The management committee should receive it officially at their meeting (which the auditor may attend) and make sure that all the points are followed up. If there are a lot of recommendations, it is useful to prioritise them as 'urgent', or 'important', or 'less important' and then start by implementing the urgent ones.

An audit report

This is a formal document which expresses the 'auditor's opinion' (see Box 10). It may draw attention to limitations in the scope of the audit (see paragraph 2 of Box 10). A negative or 'qualified' audit report may highlight a disagreement in the accounting treatment of a particular item which the organisation has not fully explained (see paragraph 3 in Box 11). The 'except for' sentence (paragraph 4 of Box 11) suggests that apart from this one item, the accounting statements are not misleading. This opinion would be more strongly stated if the financial statements as a whole were misleading.

The audit report is attached to the annual accounting statements and circulated to donors and other stakeholders. It can also be used as a fund-raising tool and given to potential donors.

Box 10: Example of an audit report with no negative comments ('unqualified' audit report)[4]

We have audited the accounting records of the Lomtaka Health Care Centre, together with the financial statements for the year ended 31 December. These have been prepared in accordance with the accounting policies shown in the notes to the accounts. The audit was conducted in accordance with generally accepted auditing standards.

As with many similar organisations of this size, the procedures of internal control rely on the close involvement of the Centre's management. We have accepted the assurance of the Centre's management that there has been appropriate authorisation and incurring of expenditure for the benefit of the Centre. Funds raised as a result of voluntary donations cannot be verified until they appear in the Centre's accounting records.

The financial statements have been prepared in accordance with National Accounting Standards. In our opinion the accounts present a true and fair view of the state of the Lomtaka Health Care Centre's affairs for the year ended 31 December.

....
Auditors

Date: ....

Box 11: Example of an audit report with a negative comment ('qualified' audit report)[4]

We have audited the accounting records of the Lomtaka Health Care Centre, together with the financial statements for the year ended 31 December. These have been prepared in accordance with the accounting policies shown in the notes to the accounts. The audit was conducted in accordance with generally accepted auditing standards.

As with many similar organisations of this size, the procedures of internal control rely on the close involvement of the Centre's management. We have accepted the assurance of the Centre's management that there has been appropriate authorisation and incurring of expenditure for the benefit of the Centre. Funds raised as a result of voluntary donations cannot be verified until they appear in the Centre's accounting records.

While conducting the audit, we have found examples of grant income received which has not, in our opinion, been used for the purpose for which it was given. These items were not accounted for in a way that we would normally expect of an organisation of this type.

The financial statements have been prepared in accordance with National Accounting Standards. Except for the comment in the previous paragraph, in our opinion the accounts present a true and fair view of the state of the Lomtaka Health Care Centre's affairs for the year ended 31 December.

....
Auditors

Date: ....

How to find an auditor

Sometimes it is not easy to find a suitable auditor, especially one who has experience of dealing with non-profit organisations. You could ask for a recommendation from other organisations, or from donors, who sometimes keep a list of accounting firms and partnerships, or go directly to a local accounting firm – but ask for references from their clients in non-profit organisations, and follow them up.

Box 12: External audit – common concerns

Concerns	Possible solutions
No audit takes place in our organisation.	Check whether an audit is legally required. If so, find an auditor, not forgetting to include the fee in the budget. (Donors will often pay for this.) If not, ask your organisation if an external audit would be beneficial for building capacity. If so, arrange it.
An auditor is needed, but we don't know where to find a good one.	Ask similar organisations, or your donors. Standards vary, so it is important to meet the auditor who will do the audit (not just the firm's partner), to discuss the kind of approach they will take. Ask, for example, *'Do you provide a management audit?'*, *'What would a management audit involve?'*, *'How long will the audit take?'*, and *'May I speak to some of your clients?'*
Our management committee do not appoint the external auditor.	Include 'appointment of auditor' on the management committee's agenda each year, well in advance of the end of the year.
The same auditor has been with our organisation for 20 years. Everybody knows her and likes her.	It is difficult to be objective after so long, especially if the auditor is liked. If there are other auditors available locally, think about changing. If not possible, see if another auditor from the same firm could do the audit.

Box continues overleaf

Concerns	Possible solutions
Auditors only look at our financial records, never at the systems or impact of the work.	Decide what you want from an audit. For all but small organisations, it is important to audit financial and management systems, as well as financial records. This will provide recommendations for building financial management capacity. Some auditors are also willing to assess the impact of your work, but you will need to ask them to do this.
Our audit is always done by the auditors' junior staff; the senior staff don't get involved until the very end.	This tends to be usual, as it reduces the costs. If you think this is affecting the quality of the audit, talk with the auditors' senior staff or think about changing the auditors.
Our auditor provides an 'audit report', but never gives us any recommendations.	Ask the auditor to provide recommendations at the end of every audit.
Our auditor provides only verbal recommendations.	Ask the auditor to put the recommendations in writing.
Our auditor's recommendations are never taken seriously.	If the recommendations are seen only by the management committee, examine the minutes and find out what happens to the recommendations after the meeting. Paid staff or volunteers should be responsible for following up each point. The management committee should insist on receiving progress reports at each meeting, until all the recommendations are implemented.
We have an annual external audit, but both our donors want to send their own auditors.	Ask the donors if your external audit report would be enough for their purposes. If not, welcome the donors' auditors as well.

8 | Organisational aspects of financial management

In this chapter we identify five organisational aspects that can either help or hinder financial management capacity-building. These (outlined in Figure 2 on page 11) are the management committee, finance staff, financial information, organisational culture, and external relationships.

Organisational aspects: the management committee

Some members of the management committee may be unaware of their responsibility for the quality of the financial side of their organisation. In some countries it is a legal requirement. The tasks that they need to consider in order to fulfil this responsibility include the following:

- Setting objectives
- Approving and regularly monitoring the budget
- Approving the annual accounting statements
- Appointing the auditors
- Receiving and acting on the audit report
- Making sure there is adequate money and funding to continue
- Appointing adequate finance staff
- Ensuring a high standard of financial management
- Reporting to donors on what has been received
- Complying with national legislation and regulations

Members of the management committee in smaller organisations may be involved in the day-to-day financial tasks, but in many organisations they are not. It is essential therefore that one member is specifically responsible for looking after the financial side of their work and bringing regular reports and decisions to the whole management committee.

You need as a minimum someone who is honest and numerate, who shares the organisation's values (for example, its commitment to diversity and gender equality), and who will work with others to achieve the aims of the organisation. Finding a suitable finance person can sometimes be difficult. Ideally, he or she should be someone with experience of dealing with financial matters. For larger organisations this could be a qualified accountant. Where it is not possible to find anyone suitable, some organisations advertise within their own and other known organisations; or consult their donors; or find a staff member from another organisation; or train an existing member. Alternatively, a member takes on the role but works with a paid person who provides advice. Or someone is paid (if allowed by national law) to act as an adviser to the management committee rather than a member of it.

Someone may be appointed who has the practical skills but no previous experience of working with a non-profit organisation. It is important then to make sure that training is available to help the person to understand and fit into the organisational culture as quickly as possible.

This financial responsibility of the management committee must be fulfilled. Organisations which do not have someone giving this advice to the senior decision-making body are less likely to be sustainable.

Understanding the information

The management committee have a controlling and questioning role, so members must have a basic understanding of what they are seeing in financial reports. At least one or two members should ask questions (for example: '*Why have we not spent the budgeted amount on materials?*' or '*Will our donor still pay for this item, even though it's overspent?*') If they do not ask questions, finance staff or an external facilitator may need to make the information clearer and train members in interpreting it.

The management committee have a key role in controlling the organisation. The financial information can highlight major problems, for example:

- There is not enough money to pay the bills.
- We need more donor funding.
- Our programme is not operating as expected.
- Money may have been stolen.

If the management committee are not using the financial information, the leader or managers must ask themselves why not. In the immediate future the leader or manager must take the necessary action themselves.

Finance sub-committees

Larger organisations usually have a separate 'finance sub-committee' which takes responsibility for many of the financial tasks. This sub-committee might include members of the management committee and staff. It will have more time to look at the details. But even where a sub-committee exists, the management committee still needs a full report at each meeting and makes decisions such as approving the budget, appointing the auditors, and receiving the audit report.

Organisational aspects: finance staff

It is important that finance volunteers and paid staff are trained to do their job competently or are experienced. Different-sized organisations need different skills, for example:

- **A group of volunteers:** at least one experienced member responsible for finance.

- **Small to medium-sized organisations:** one paid member of staff with a job description that defines finance as either part or all of their job. This person may not be a financial expert, but some of the work needs professional accounting skills. One option is to use an accountant for work such as the end-of-year accounting statements: someone who is either employed on a part-time basis or hired from a firm of local accountants.

- **Medium-sized to large organisations:** a book-keeper (someone keeping the accounting records) is appointed, capable of accounting of a more technical nature. In these organisations, someone other than the book-keeper may be responsible for other financial tasks, for example handing out cash (which is the job of a 'cashier').

- **Large organisations:** with more complex accounting systems, there is usually at least one accountant (sometimes called a 'financial controller') who has qualified for the role by taking professional accounting exams. He or she is usually a member of a recognised accounting institute, either in their home country or abroad.

The level of staffing depends on the complexity of your activities. Organisations working with several donors and community groups are likely to need more financial staff. Lists of typical financial tasks and necessary qualifications and experience are shown in Tables 3 and 4.

Table 3: Typical financial tasks

Tasks	Cashier	Book-keeper	Accountant / Financial Controller
Cash and bank handling			
Be responsible for office cash and keeping it safe.	✔		
Issue petty cash to team members, based on authorised documents.	✔		
Keep a record of all petty cash issued, with supporting vouchers.	✔		
Issue advances to team members, based on documents which have been authorised by the correct person.	✔		
Keep a record of advances and account for them.	✔		
File vouchers for all money coming in and money going out.	✔		
Pay wages to national staff.	✔		
Notify book-keeper/programme manager when a further amount of cash is needed.	✔		
Prepare cheques from invoices and payment requests.	✔		
Book-keeping			
Keep a cash book and update it regularly.		✔	
Make sure adequate documentation is available to support all income and expenditure.		✔	
Make sure income and expenditure are coded accurately.		✔	
Prepare wages for national staff.		✔	
Agree the bank statements with the cash book, at least monthly.		✔	
Prepare monthly summary of accounts.		✔	
Provide monthly cash flow reports.		✔	
Receive and summarise expenditure of team members.		✔	
Make sure transfers between accounts are correct.		✔	
Get explanations for items not accounted for satisfactorily.		✔	
Help the programme manager in budgeting.		✔	
Provide regular 'budget and actual' information for budget managers so that they can monitor expenditure.			✔
Provide reports on income and expenditure as required.			✔
Train team members in accounting for expenditure.			✔
Keep a record of all fixed assets.			✔

Tasks	Cashier	Book-keeper	Accountant / Financial Controller
Accounting/financial control			
Review and introduce new accounting and financial control systems.			✔
Manage accounting staff.			✔
Count the cash held by the cashier regularly and agree with the accounting records.			✔
Manage the funds in the bank account(s) including transfers.			✔
Maintain a strong business relationship with bankers.			✔
Monitor the cash advances system.			✔
Visit programmes to provide advice on accounting and financial control systems.			✔
Look at the accounting implications for any new programme proposal, before it is submitted for funding.			✔
Make sure that programme managers prepare programme and administrative budgets. Provide technical support where needed.			✔
Meet with programme managers to make sure budgets are adequately monitored.			✔
Arrange production of other management information, as required.			✔
Communicate with donors to make sure that their reporting requirements can be fulfilled.			✔
Provide accurate reports to donors in their required format when they want them.			✔
Audit operational projects and arrange for external audit as required.			✔
Make sure audit recommendations are discussed and implemented.			✔
Provide training in accounting for programme staff and other team members.			✔
Interpret financial information for non-accountants.			✔

Notes

1. In smaller programmes, where only one 'financial' member of staff is employed, some tasks will need to be given to other staff, e.g. the cashiering role.

2. The person who prepares cheques should not be a cheque signatory. If several finance staff members are employed the most senior may sign cheques along with the programme manager, providing they are not involved in the day-to-day cheque preparation. If there is only one finance person, cheque signing should be the responsibility of the programme manager with another signatory.

Source: 'Financial Management for Emergencies' © www.fme-online.org[5]

Table 4: Qualifications and experience of finance staff

	Cashier	Book-keeper	Accountant / Financial Controller
Experience of the tasks on the job description, see Typical Tasks	Essential	Essential	Essential
Numerate, methodical and accurate	Essential	Essential	Essential
Honest and trustworthy	Essential	Essential	Essential
Familiarity with both an accounting package and Excel, indicating an ability to learn the organisation's accounting software, if different		Essential	Essential
Experience of recruiting staff and providing one-to-one training			Essential
Supervisory and management experience			Essential
Experience of setting up financial systems in emergencies			Essential
Able to communicate effectively both verbally and in writing			Essential
Formal accounting qualification			Highly desirable

Source: 'Financial Management for Emergencies' © www.fme-online.org[5]

Financial structures

In addition to recruiting and developing financial staff, organisations need to have clear management structures. If there is only one finance person, it is important to set clear boundaries and have a clear reporting line, especially if this member of staff is relatively junior. For example, this person needs to know if he or she is expected to represent financial matters at planning discussions and to be involved in the management's longer-term planning for the organisation.

In larger organisations there may be a hierarchical structure. The senior member of the finance team would normally have formal training or an accounting qualification. He or she would usually take part in longer-term planning and decision-making for the organisation. It is important to have clear job descriptions for financial staff, and for this senior staff member to build the capacity of the finance team. The structure should always show a clear 'separation of duties' (see Chapter 6, p.46).

Story: Using financial skills

Asylum Welcome was founded about 10 years ago by a group of volunteers to provide support through advice and practical help for the increased numbers of refugees and asylum seekers in the UK. In the early days the voluntary treasurer was responsible for all the financial work. Office accommodation was provided free of charge in a community hall, and volunteers provided the advice work. There were minimal transactions. Individuals and local groups contributed funds.

After about four years, the work had grown. A number of organisations provided funds, staff had been appointed, and the organisation rented its own premises. The services expanded to work with families and young people.

The accounting needs also increased. The voluntary treasurer still did some of the day-to-day financial work, and a qualified accountant was employed for half a day a week to complete the office accounting and budget reports. This made good use of the accountant's skills and was not too expensive. The accountant also prepared the year-end accounting statements. This was cheaper than using a firm of accountants. Volunteers helped with some of the routine financial tasks.

As the organisation grew further, in addition to the part-time accountant, a financial assistant was employed for half a day each week to reconcile petty cash, record donations, and write cheques. This freed up the voluntary treasurer to concentrate on the financial policy issues.

(Asylum Welcome, United Kingdom)

Professional training for finance staff

Non-profit organisations often cannot afford to employ highly trained or qualified staff. One alternative is to train staff who deal with financial matters and so build individual and organisational capacity. Some training is 'on the job', but training courses are often available and may be more appropriate. They are sometimes provided by donors or 'umbrella organisations', and sometimes commercially. Ideally the training will be specific to the needs of the non-profit sector.

Some medium-sized and large organisations provide funding and/or time for their staff to study for professional accounting qualifications. The organisation then benefits from their increased skills and motivation, often at a lower cost than recruiting a qualified accountant. Training agreements often require the person concerned to work for the organisation for a certain number of years after qualifying. In reality, this can be difficult to enforce. Another way is to make sure that you do not invest everything in only one person, but look for ways to spread the benefits of that individual's training throughout the whole organisation (see 'Maximising the learning' in Chapter 12).

Communication about financial matters

Clear communication about financial issues strengthens the financial management capacity of a group or organisation. It affects every part of an organisation, for example:

- The members of the management committee need information and need to have their questions answered in a non-technical way.
- The leader and managers need appropriate information and explanations to understand financial statements and what they mean for the organisation.
- Programme and finance staff need to make sure that the information is detailed enough for programme management and for donors.
- Beneficiaries, communities, partners, and donors need clear, concise financial information and advice that they can understand.

In practice, weaknesses may occur, for the following reasons:

- Programme staff think that finance staff do not understand their work, and vice versa.
- Financial jargon and technical language are used and not understood.
- 'Finance' is thought to be a matter for specialists.
- Good communication skills are ignored when recruiting finance staff.
- Financial management skills are ignored when recruiting programme staff.

Achieving better financial communication

Finance people are not primarily recruited for their communication skills, but they need to communicate clearly, concisely, and in an encouraging way. This applies to all groups and organisations at whatever level: to the finance person on the management committee, to paid staff, and indeed to anyone who is talking about finance. Without these skills, an organisation's financial management capacity is reduced, because people think that finance is only for specialists and no one else need bother. Good communication will enhance financial management skills, resulting in a more effective programme which attracts more donors. Always encourage the best practice, as shown in Box 13.

An excellent way of improving communication is to arrange regular budget-monitoring meetings between finance and non-finance staff. Whenever a budget and actual statement or donor report is produced, arrange to have a short meeting soon afterwards to clarify the reports and discuss any concerns.

Box 13: Best practice in financial communications

Do

- Be clear and concise.
- Focus on the key points.
- Use simple language.
- See the issue from the other person's point of view.
- Watch out for people losing interest; ask them 'Is this making sense?'
- Give plenty of opportunity for them to ask questions.
- Encourage people to ask for more information.
- Work with others to improve the clarity of financial information and systems.

Don't

- Use technical terms before explaining what they mean in everyday language.
- Talk for too long – a few minutes is enough.
- Confuse people with financial concepts and jargon.

Story: Short, regular meetings

Programme and finance staff were finding it difficult to understand each other. Programme staff needed support from finance staff; and finance staff needed to be able to understand the needs of the programme and provide appropriate information.

A series of one-to-one meetings was arranged between managers and the finance member of staff dealing with their project. These meetings are held monthly to coincide with the production of budget and actual and donor reports. They usually last less than 30 minutes. In addition, a monthly meeting of all finance and programme staff is held to talk about common concerns. We wonder whether meeting every two months might be enough for these larger meetings. The meetings make it possible to share problems and plan the way forward.

There is now greater mutual understanding. Finance people appreciate how difficult it can be to obtain the necessary paperwork required by donors, and they have started to consider whether there are other ways of meeting donors' requirements. Programme people have started to appreciate the difficulties of producing the financial reports required, and some have become experts in finance! It is hoped to develop the relationship further by arranging field visits for finance staff, and to continue financial training for programme staff.

(Cini Asha, India)

Write clearly

Documents for non-finance staff should be written simply and avoid using any technical language. It takes time to develop these writing skills, but if you want people to understand what you are saying and act on it, it can make a big difference. Rules for writing in this style are shown in Box 14.

Box 14: How to write clearly

- Plan before you write.
- Organise the information into sections.
- Avoid technical language or jargon words, or at least explain them.
- Use positive rather than negative phrases: write *'The cash/bank book will be much easier to control if it is updated regularly'* rather than *'If the cash/bank book is not updated regularly, it can be more difficult to control'.*
- Use 'active' rather than 'passive' language: write *'We will complete the cash/bank book'* rather than *'The cash/bank book will be completed'.*
- Turn nouns into verbs: write *'Your manager will decide if s/he will reimburse travel expenses'* rather than *'All decisions about the reimbursement of travel expenses are judged by your manager'.*
- Be concise and limit sentences to no more than 15–20 words.
- Have only one main idea for each sentence.

Other ways of developing the capacity of finance staff

Interviews and tests

When recruiting staff with specific financial responsibilities, set a test based on the kind of work they will have to do. Candidates for the job of a finance person could be asked to agree the organisation's own bank records with the bank statement. The test will be one factor in making the selection. Not doing well in the test will not always mean rejecting the candidate. However, if such a person is appointed, you will be aware of the need for financial training.

'Sector' skills

Finance people may not have worked in a non-commercial organisation before. The culture of a non-profit organisation may be quite different, and it is important for everyone that they feel settled quickly. Issues such as gender equality and social diversity may be new to them, and they may need training. It is vital that the decisions that finance staff make, for example in budgeting, are in accordance with organisational priorities.

Programme visits

The role of finance people is often limited in scope. Although the organisation has an exciting programme of activities, they may never see examples of it. Make sure that there are some opportunities for finance staff to visit the programme. This can increase their understanding of the pressures that programme people face.

Organisational aspects: financial information

Up-to-date and accurate financial information is essential for managing the activities of any group and organisation. Organisations with paper-based systems need well-trained finance people to help them to keep good records and produce clear financial reports.

For computerised organisations, hardware and/or software may be out of date, and may not produce what you need. Donors may help you to upgrade and may pay for training staff in a new system. If information is always out of date, it is also worth looking at other factors. For example: are there enough staff to provide the level of service you need? Or is there a 'blockage' that prevents inputting of information?

If the financial system is designed primarily for accountants, others may not understand the information. Financial reports must be 'user-friendly' so that readers can understand them, feel competent to question them, and take the necessary decisions.

See also 'Who needs to build budgeting capacity?' in Chapter 3.

Organisational aspects: organisational culture

The role of the leadership team

Members of the management committee and the leader influence how finance is dealt with across an organisation. If it is treated as a low priority (*'The finance team are wonderful and deal with everything financial, which leaves me able to concentrate on the programme'*), you may lose the positive aspects that financial management can offer an organisation and its programme. If managers are saying '*It is not my responsibility and I don't want to get involved*' (and possibly '*I don't understand it*'), this can lead to a lack of control over financial matters and therefore poorer funding prospects.

An organisation that treats finance as a high priority ('*We all understand the importance of finance here; the finance team are great, and my responsibility is to be financially informed, which helps me to take better decisions*'), there will be a positive impact on people throughout the organisation.

The leadership team, and especially the leader, need to give a consistent message that finance is important. The message must be supported by good financial behaviour from the leader, for example completing a tour-expenses form as soon as they return from a trip.

A change in the leadership's message about finance can, very quickly, influence an organisation's culture, either positively or negatively. This message needs to be constantly reinforced.

Story: A leader's influence

Everyone was excited when a new director arrived at a well-run organisation. The organisation had ten members of staff, most of whom worked with community groups to build their capacity. It had excellent financial and management systems and a number of long-term donors.

The new director had many ideas of how the programme work could be developed, and these were introduced with great success. She was, however, not interested in managing the organisation; she delegated every responsibility that was not directly related to the programme. She would praise administrative staff for their contribution, and was often heard to say that she did not need to check the finances because *we have a talented and trustworthy administrator*. This meant that the administrator made financial decisions which should have been made by the director. No one bothered to monitor budgets or check that donor reporting was up to date. Financial controls were not applied, and requests for payments were authorised by senior staff without knowing what they were signing for.

After eighteen months, the organisation faced serious problems. First, two long-standing donors withdrew their funding, saying that its financial management was not up to the required standard. Second, the administrator had stolen money from the organisation over six months and no one had noticed until the annual external audit. The administrator was dismissed, with a lot of negative publicity. The programme had to be reduced dramatically, and the future of the organisation became very uncertain.

(From training workshops in Asia and Europe)

Non-finance staff

Non-finance staff often need basic financial management skills to do their job. Programme staff, for example, working with beneficiaries, community groups, and partners, may be asked to help them to prepare a budget, keep a record of money coming in and going out, operate a bank account, and present a report on what has been spent. Staff in these situations should be able to advise confidently, but also to recognise the limits of their knowledge. You may sometimes need to say '*This is beyond my expertise and I need to ask someone else to help*'.

Box 15 lists some questions to ask about the working relationships between programme and finance staff.

Financial training

Training for non-finance people can improve their understanding of financial matters. Sometimes finance people within the organisation can provide it; if not, you need to bring in an outside facilitator. Such a training event in itself can raise the profile of finance as well as build the capacity of non-finance staff.

Recruitment

When recruiting non-finance staff whose jobs include financial responsibilities, you should include a numerical test, such as comparing a budget and actual statement (similar to the example in Chapter 3) and suggesting points to follow up.

Box 15: Questions about working relationships between programme and finance staff

- Does the leader give finance a high priority?
- Does the leader complete his/her personal financial returns on time?
- Do finance and programme staff meet regularly to discuss monthly/quarterly budgets and/or donor reports?
- Is financial training available for non-finance staff?
- Do finance staff have opportunities to visit programme activities?
- Are finance staff involved when new programmes are planned?
- Are finance staff encouraged to avoid using jargon when talking to non-finance people?
- Is at least one person able to communicate about finance with non-finance people in a way that they understand?
- Do interviews for programme staff dealing with financial work include a practical numerical test?
- Do chairs of meetings regularly ask *'What are the financial implications of this decision?'*
- Are finance staff given opportunities to contribute effectively to the organisation's objectives?
- Where are the desks of the finance and programme staff in relation to each other?

Organisational aspects: external relationships

Organisations need to relate well to a range of 'stakeholders': groups and individuals, internal or external, who have an interest in the organisation's well-being. They include:

- beneficiaries, community groups, and partner organisations
- donors
- paid staff and volunteers
- suppliers of goods and services
- local and national government.

Key financial relationships exist with the first two of these stakeholders: beneficiaries and donors.

Beneficiaries

It is important to inform your beneficiaries about the financial position of your organisation. Tell them what it means for the priorities of their community. This will help to increase the participation of beneficiaries in the activities that you are running, which may strengthen the impact of the programme.

Find appropriate ways of telling your beneficiaries how you plan to use money that you have allocated to them, and later how you actually used it. For example:

- Use a flipchart or whiteboard to present the key areas of your budget.
- Include a bar chart or pie diagram in a programme newsletter to show where the money has come from and where it has gone to. Computer spreadsheet programmes can easily convert figures into diagrams.
- Draw a flipchart poster with similar details that can be displayed where beneficiaries gather.
- Give out printed copies of financial information, summarised on no more than one page, following the best practice in communicating financial information. See Box 13.
- Call a meeting to discuss financial priorities and what they mean for their community.
- Ensure that materials are translated into the languages used.

Make sure that women and poorer members of the community are not left out of the discussions. If you are working in a community where gender issues are very sensitive, you may, for example, need to find ways of reaching the female members of the community by perhaps using a female facilitator.

If you are working with partner groups, their financial management capacity can be linked to yours. Funding is often given as part of a chain. Reporting back from one partner to another must be done well. The original donor is more likely to continue funding if you submit adequate financial reports. Many of the ideas in this book can be applied to organisations of any size. Share them with your partner organisations, and help them to build their capacity too.

Donors

Many organisations rely on external funding to continue their programme. One aspect of building financial management capacity is to have a strong relationship with donors. You need to have a commitment from them to fund your programme over several years, if possible. Donors can in practice be a catalyst for building your capacity, by demanding a high standard of financial reporting and providing financial management capacity-building inputs. These inputs may include an invitation to attend workshops that the donor provides or funds; 'on the job training' for finance staff; funds for external audits; and advice about the kinds of system that might be appropriate.

What could go wrong?

However well an organisation is running, it is necessary to consider what could go wrong. This is often part of longer-term planning. Larger organisations sometimes call this 'planning for risks'. These include the withdrawal of donor funding, political changes, or new national legislation. Risks may be external and out of your control, or internal, for example key staff (paid or voluntary) leaving without warning. Larger organisations often have formal risk policies, but all organisations must ask the following questions:

- What could go wrong?
- How likely is it to happen?
- What impact would it have?
- What can we do to prevent it?
- What would we do if it happened?
- Would any of these events mean that we could not continue?

Asking the questions and thinking about the consequences helps to protect an organisation from the many uncertainties that they face. The management committee and staff need to discuss these issues at least once each year.

What are 'risks'?

'A risk is a potentially damaging outcome of an event or situation, which could be internal or external to the organisation. It could have major or minor effects, or it could have none. A responsible organisation anticipates the risks involved in its work, makes well-considered decisions on how to address them, and ensures that it acts on those decisions to protect the people who could be put at risk and the organisation itself.'[6]

Box 16: Organisational aspects of financial management – common concerns

Concerns	Possible solutions
We are a rural organisation with no access to professional accounting skills. We are not able to use computers very often.	First decide what accounting records and reports you need, by talking with donors and stakeholders. Some organisations only need paper-based basic accounting. Systems can usually be designed to provide what you need with the skills and resources that you have, perhaps with some outside help from time to time.
No one is responsible for finance at the meetings of our management committee. They don't think they need anyone.	Someone must prioritise the financial side of the work. Convince members of the importance of this. Propose someone to join the committee who is willing to take on the role, or suggest one of the existing members.
Only the management committee finance person understands our budget and actual reports.	Improve the clarity of the information given to the management committee. Train members to interpret the information and ask questions.

Concerns	Possible solutions
Are we large enough to have a finance sub-committee?	If there is not enough time to deal with financial issues at the meetings of the management committee, consider appointing a finance sub-committee which would have more time to go into details. However, don't let this be a reason for not discussing finance at the main management committee meetings. All its members are still responsible.
Accountants are expensive and hard to recruit. We are a small organisation and can't afford someone with the right qualifications.	Divide the work between routine tasks and professional work. Think about a part-time person for the professional work, and see if you can absorb the routine tasks into other jobs. Consider recruiting someone at a lower level and supporting him or her through professional training.
I can't understand our finance manager. He talks in jargon.	A two-way approach is needed. You need to find help in understanding some of the jargon; the finance manager needs help to communicate better. Start by sharing the advice in Boxes 13 and 14.
Our finance staff say that the software we are using is not suitable for what we need, but we can't afford anything better.	If you have donors, talk with them about this. They may be willing to fund new software. Don't forget to add the cost of training for staff to the budget. Old software that cannot give up-to-date and 'user-friendly' financial information can lead to poorly managed programmes.

Concerns	Possible solutions
Our leader doesn't understand financial issues and covers it up by getting other people to do everything.	Leaders must have a working knowledge of finance and understand its importance. Confidential financial management training for the leader from an outside facilitator may help them to develop without losing face.
Programme staff are often asked for financial advice, but don't feel confident to give it.	Arrange some training in basic financial management for staff. Either find a suitable course for non-profit organisations; or, if possible, arrange your own training. Use your finance people, or ask an outside facilitator to help. Put the cost of this in your next budget.
Our management committee only look at current issues, never at the future.	Arrange a special meeting to consider longer-term issues. Start by thinking about possible 'risks' and ways to deal with them.

Part 3 | Moving Towards Sustainability

9 | Reserves

In earlier chapters we have considered the skills, systems, and organisational factors that are needed to build financial management capacity. The next two chapters look at different, but equally important areas. Reserves and core costs are vital in helping an organisation to move towards achieving financial sustainability. This chapter explains what reserves are, whether your organisation needs them, how to calculate an appropriate level, and practical ways of building them up. It also considers the use of a 'reserves policy' and explains how thinking about reserves may make a useful contribution to keeping your organisation going in the long term.

Many non-profit organisations need donors to fund their work so that they can continue their activities. If, however, there is not enough funding for a particular year, an organisation can sometimes use some of its savings – or 'reserves' – from previous years.

Reserve funds are the 'unrestricted' money (that is not allocated to a particular programme), over and above the money that an organisation receives and spends in a particular year. They can be seen as 'organisational savings'. Reserves are 'that part of a charity's income funds that is freely available'.[7] Some organisations describe reserves as 'funds' (see Box 17). They act as a safety net in case income suddenly drops or expenditure increases.

Stories: What are 'reserves'?

A personal story

In my first year of work I received a salary of 10,500. My expenses for rent, travel to work, food, and entertainment cost me 9,750. I put 750 into my savings account.

The second year I again received 10,500 as salary, but in addition to my expenses of 9,750 I had to pay health costs of a further 1,000 – a total of 10,750. I took the extra 250 that I needed from my savings. It left 500 in my savings account.

An organisation's story

In the first year we started, we had 10,500 from donations. Our project expenses, travel, newsletter production, and meetings came to 9,750. We put 750 into our savings account.

The second year we again received 10,500 and paid our expenses of 9,750; but this year we also had a new health project costing 1,000 more – a total of 10,750. We took the extra 250 from our savings account. We were still able to keep 500 in our savings account. We started to call the money in our savings account our 'reserves'. We do not need it yet, but we may do in future years.

(From a training workshop, Lebanon)

Do you need to worry about reserves?

Some organisations have no reserves and spend all that they receive, each year. Some find that building up reserves is impossible, because they rarely receive unrestricted funds and it is difficult to raise more funds. Some do not really need to hold reserves: groups or organisations with no paid staff, premises, or on-going commitments can manage without additional money to act as their 'safety net'. If they run out of money, they either stop working, or pay for what they need themselves.

In countries where there is a medium to high inflation rate, holding money in the bank does not help an organisation. Also, in some countries banks do not pay interest on an organisation's deposited money. This is because inflation can absorb the savings that have been put aside as reserves. In such countries, if the law allows, surplus money is sometimes used to purchase items that will not decrease in value, for example a building whose rent is used as income for the organisation. If this is not possible, organisations usually do not keep reserves.

However, in most countries organisations with paid staff, premises, and commitments to beneficiaries must hold some reserves. As an organisation grows, it needs to consider whether it would be able to continue if some or all of its funding stopped, and whether it is essential that its services continue to be provided. If so, the organisation needs reserves.

Box 17: Different types of funds

Restricted funds ('earmarked', 'tied' or 'ring-fenced')

Money given by a donor for a particular purpose. The funds can only be used for that purpose. They cannot be used to create a reserve fund.

Unrestricted funds ('free money' or 'general purpose income')

Money given by a donor for general use or raised by the organisation itself, for example through membership fees or local fundraising.

Designated funds

Unrestricted money that the management committee has set aside for a particular purpose, for example for repairs to premises in a future year. These funds must be 'designated' for this purpose by the management committee. They can be 'undesignated' later, but only by the management committee.

Endowment funds (or 'corpus funds')

Money given by a donor (or sometimes saved from previous year's surpluses) that the organisation invests in order to provide interest for running costs. 'Permanent' endowments allow only the interest of the fund to be used, not the fund itself. 'Expendable' endowments are funds that the management committee can either invest or convert into income. These funds can be either restricted or unrestricted, depending on the donor.

General funds (or 'income and expenditure account')

Money still held from the current year and the previous year's surpluses.

Why hold reserves?

Reserves are held for several purposes:

- To provide for times when money due is received after money paid.
- To enable work to continue if income/fund-raising is not as high as expected.
- To provide time to make savings or raise funds if money expected is not received or is received late.
- To be able to spend money that has not been planned or budgeted, if an opportunity or emergency arises.

It is important to find out what is actually included as 'reserves'. The savings built up over previous years may, for example, be in the bank account, but may still not be available to spend. They may have been given by donors for a particular purpose and they will only allow it to be spent on that. Or if savings are invested in a building or equipment, this money too may not be readily available to spend.

The level of reserves

It can be difficult to decide the level of reserves that an organisation needs. For example, donors may not give funds if they think that an organisation is holding too much money in reserve. But if too little is held, the management committee may be putting the organisation's future at risk.

Each organisation has different needs, and the level of reserves will depend on its type and size. For example, a small organisation with few staff and secure funding may need only low reserves. A larger organisation offering a changing range of services, which has a large staff and which finds it difficult to get enough funding each year, needs higher reserves. A list of factors to consider when deciding on the level of reserves to hold is shown in Box 18.

Box 18: Factors to consider when deciding the level of reserves

- Whether you are required by law or by donors to hold reserves.
- The effect on beneficiaries if you were unable to provide the services.
- The range and reliability of income sources.
- The proportions of 'restricted' and 'unrestricted' income.
- Current and expected future plans and levels of expenditure.
- The sensitivity of income and expenditure to outside influences, for example government rules.
- The value of outstanding commitments.
- The level at which reserves may discourage donors from providing further funding.
- Whether the current reserves are in bank or cash, or invested in buildings and equipment.
- The size of any investments.
- Your ability to respond quickly to changing circumstances, and the time it would take to raise more funds.
- The amount of 'unrestricted' money that is raised through any membership fees, donations, and local fundraising.

Reserves policy

For organisations which have regular commitments, employ staff, and have their own offices, it is best practice to produce a written policy on reserves. It should include the following items:

- the reason for keeping reserves
- the level of reserves needed
- how this level will be achieved/maintained
- how often the policy is reviewed.

Reserves policies are often expressed as either a proportion of income or a proportion of expenditure. They could also be expressed as a time period, for example '50 per cent or six months of budgeted expenditure'. This means that if all funding stopped, the reserves would be enough to pay for activities for a further six months. This would provide time for more fund-raising. Policies are usually reviewed annually, or at least every few years. An example of a reserves policy is shown in Box 19.

The policy may be drafted by a member of staff, or an organisation's auditor, or a professional accountant, but it is the management committee's responsibility to approve it and make sure that it is in place. The policy should be included in the annual report and accounts, thereby demonstrating that the organisation is acting openly in justifying the level of reserves to its stakeholders.

Perhaps the main benefit of having a policy is to allow those responsible to think through and plan how they would keep the organisation going if they could not raise enough funds. Planning for an appropriate level of reserves, even if it is not achievable immediately, shows that you are managing your organisation in a responsible way. And it is a contribution towards making the organisation sustainable.

Box 19: Example of a reserves policy

Santé needs to keep reserves to cover changes in fundraising and so that we can continue to provide on-going services to our clients. We aim to hold reserves at 35 per cent, or just over four months, of our expenditure budget. This target should be achieved over the next three years. It will be in place by 31 December ... The management committee will then review this percentage annually when the budget is being set.

Story: A reserves policy

The Centre for the Study of Violence and Reconciliation was founded in 1989.

We were concerned that the Centre did not have a policy on reserves, and the money that it did hold could give donors the impression that it did not need their funding. A policy would explain to funders and supporters why it was necessary for the Centre to hold money, rather than spend it all, even though the reserves were only to be used for times when there were delays in receiving grants or funding was short.

We felt that writing a policy would help us to plan better, would support the fundraising effort, and would improve the allocation of resources. The reserves would have to be built up over a period, for example from surplus unrestricted funds or from income-generating projects.

We needed the level of reserves to be high enough to allow us to deal with temporary downturns in fundraising without having to reduce programme expenditure. We knew that some organisations calculate reserves as being three months of either salaries or total operating expenditure. We calculated both. In the end we were recommended to base the amount on three months' operating costs and to build up to this gradually. Any interest from the reserves held would contribute towards our running costs.

The policy will be approved by the board and published in the Centre's procedures manual and annual financial statements and report. Once established, the policy and the amount will be reviewed regularly, at least every three years.

(Centre for the Study of Violence and Reconciliation, South Africa)

Methods of building up reserves

It can be difficult to build up reserves. Here are two suggestions:

- **Talk with your donor.** Some donors will say they will not fund reserves; if so, accept their decision and move on. Other donors understand the issue, will discuss your policy with you, and may make helpful suggestions. It is certainly acceptable to approach donors. Some organisations feel embarrassed to ask – don't be! Some donors see organisations that have low reserves or no reserves as a bad risk for their funding.

- **Build up a surplus of unrestricted funds gradually.** Increase reserves to the necessary level by using some 'unrestricted' funds each year – even if only a small amount. This may involve using money from local fund-raising events, membership fees, charges for services, small donations, or income-generating projects. It may take several years to reach the level that you need, and it should be seen as an organisational objective and part of the budget-planning process.

Changes in reserves and the budget

If reserves are either to be created or increased, the income part of the budget should be greater than the expenditure for that year.

Total income	100,000
Total expenditure	98,000
Contribution to reserves	**2,000**

However, including the figures in the budget does not necessarily mean that it will happen. The management committee must regularly monitor the budget to make sure that expenditure is kept within the set limit, and that all expected income is received.

A 'deficit budget' will use up some of the existing reserves. This should be planned in advance, but only if you have some reserves to spare.

Total income	98,000
Total expenditure	100,000
Reduction in reserves	**2,000**

Box 20: Reserves – common concerns

Concerns	Possible solutions
We are a small voluntary organisation with no staff or other commitments. We raise our own funds and spend what we raise each year. Do we need reserves?	Probably not. Keep a small amount in your bank account in case you want to pay out an amount before you raise the funds. If you grow in size, or receive donor funding, think about reserves again.
Our organisation has never thought about reserves, but our beneficiaries would find it very difficult if we stopped operating.	It is worth looking at ways to build reserves, if not immediately then in the longer term. Discuss it with the management committee and decide how much would be needed to make the organisation sustainable. Think of ways to raise this amount.
All our funding is for a particular purpose, and we cannot build up any reserves from it.	Consider whether it is important for you to have reserves. If so, decide whether you can raise your own funds, maybe through local fund-raising, or a minimal charge for services, or membership fees. Talk with your donor about the possibilities.
We have reserves, but no reserves policy.	A policy is useful to explain to donors that you have thought about the issue and are managing your organisation in a professional way. Write out a draft policy, ask your management committee to discuss and approve it, and then publish it with your annual accounting statements.

10 | Core costs

In this chapter we will consider what is meant by 'core costs', and various approaches to funding these costs. One particular approach is to allocate core costs to programme budgets.

> **What are core costs?**
>
> Core costs are non-programme organisational costs. They include rent, office costs, and the salaries of administrative staff. Core costs are sometimes called 'overheads', 'administrative costs', 'indirect costs', or 'support costs'.

Donors are often unwilling to fund core costs, preferring to contribute to programme costs instead. However, the full cost of providing a programme includes the costs of the programme itself plus a proportion of core costs. If core costs are not covered, the organisation cannot be effective or financially sustainable and cannot plan for its future, or even continue. It is therefore very important to find ways of covering these costs – but this is not easy.

Core costs do not always increase in line with extra activities. For example, smaller organisations with one or two programme activities may have a relatively high level of core costs; organisations with twenty activities may be better able to spread their costs and achieve some 'economies of scale'. The cost of a vehicle is the same for all organisations, but for a smaller organisation it is a larger proportion of its costs.

The management committee are responsible for making sure that there is a plan to fund the core costs for future years.

Different stages of development

Organisations with only one activity, and one donor, may already include all their core costs in their budget and be fully funded. But funding core costs is more difficult for organisations that have more than one activity, several donors, and expenses which the budgeting and accounting do not directly link to their programme activities.

Drawing on Mike Hudson's research, Bill Bruty[8] identifies three stages of organisational development:

- **Infancy:** this is where organisations are heavily dependent on a single funding source, and growth is limited by their donor's capacity to provide more funding. Relying on one donor could limit the organisation's independence.

- **Growth phase:** as the organisation grows and becomes more independent, there is a danger of being pulled in different directions by new donors. This may not fit organisational objectives. To balance this, the organisation should aim to keep its original donors, attract a mix of new donors, and, if it can, develop its own fundraising.

- **Maturity and maintenance:** at this stage, funding should come from a changing mix of sources, to give the organisation greater security of income. A lack of accountability to donors can cause complacency in mature organisations and lead to possible decline.

Ways to fund core costs

There are a number of options, summarised below:

- **Using the 'administration allowance' from donors.** Some donors are willing to add an administrative allowance (perhaps between 5 and 20 per cent) to a grant for programme work. This is intended to cover core costs, although smaller amounts are often not enough. It is worth finding out exactly what the allowance is supposed to cover, and if it is possible to include any other administrative costs elsewhere in the programme budget.

- **Reducing core costs to a minimum.** Non-profit organisations usually run on minimum core costs, but it is worth looking at your costs and seeing if you can do the same work for less money: for example, whether there is a cheaper alternative for maintaining your computers. Use of volunteers and 'in-kind' support can help to reduce costs considerably. An occasional reminder to staff/volunteers to minimise travel, photocopying, and telephone calls might also be helpful.

- **Using your own funds and raising funds locally.** Some organisations have 'unrestricted' funds that they can use, perhaps derived from membership fees or charges for services. It may also be possible to use existing activities as a source of income. You might, for example, offer training courses to outsiders, charging them a fee and so recovering the costs of the course. It is important to manage this kind of fund-raising well, making sure that the true cost (including staff time) is not bigger than the income generated. Any proposed activities should be in line with the organisation's overall objectives and not divert staff from their main work.
- **Finding a donor that covers core costs.** These donors are unusual, and if you find one you are fortunate. Funding core costs (alone) is sometimes offered for newer organisations to help them to develop their organisational capacity.
- **Allocating core costs to programme budgets.** A proportion of core costs is allocated to the programme budgets (see below).

Accounting options

The last of the options shown above ('allocating core costs to programme budgets') can make a big difference to an organisation's funding, but it requires more accounting work to achieve it. Larger organisations often employ accountants and fund-raisers to maximise their income by including core costs with programme budgets, but smaller organisations with more than one programme activity may also consider this.

Allocating core costs to programme budgets

Your core costs could be allocated to each programme budget. If you have five programmes of an equal size, you could, for example, charge one-fifth of the office costs to each. This would move these costs away from your core-costs budget and include them in your programme budget, if it could be justified. You might argue, for example, that the office costs would not be needed unless you had the programmes.

You could take the same approach with a leader's salary, if he or she is spending time with each of the five different programmes. A proportion of the salary costs could be allocated to each programme, in proportion to the time spent. It is not usually necessary for people to keep time sheets or detailed records to determine the exact hours. Instead, an annual estimation of time spent on each programme is made and, as long as it can be justified, it is usually acceptable.

If you allocate core costs to programme budgets, three things happen:

- You see the full programme cost: your organisation can take decisions based on what a programme is really costing. For example, is this the best use of our resources, or could we do the same work for less?
- You control costs better: staff or volunteers are familiar with what everything is costing in their programme, and whether they need to reduce spending.
- You encourage 'full-cost' funding from some donors: presenting the full cost of a programme to a donor means that they are more likely to fund it and help you to recover your core costs.

This approach is sometimes called 'full-cost recovery', or 'activity-based costing'. Detailed methods for recovering core costs are outside the scope of this book but, if you need advice, you will find resources suggested in the 'Websites' and 'Further reading' sections towards the end of this book.

If you do allocate core costs to the programme, remember that donors will not cover these if they are already giving you an 'administration allowance'. Most organisations aim for a mixture of the different methods to cover their core costs. This needs careful accounting to maximise the available funding and avoid any possible double counting.

The role of finance people

You cannot assume that all finance people know how to fund core costs. This is a management issue rather than a financial issue, and someone in the leadership team may have to suggest the options. Most trained book-keepers and professional accountants will understand the principle of how to allocate core costs to programme budgets. The way in which you then present this information to donors is vital, and it is important that your finance people and those responsible for fund-raising work together. Seek professional advice about core-costs accounting, if you need it.

Story: Allocating core costs to programme budgets

Projekta is a non-profit NGO founded in 1993. We focus on building capacity in the areas of gender equality and governance.

Ensuring financial stability and funding our core costs are a major challenge. From the beginning, we have divided costs into two types: those related to the implementation of the programme activities, sometimes called 'direct costs'; and those related to core costs. The core costs were treated separately in the budget, because Projekta received financial support from a Dutch agency specifically to cover the cost of running the office.

Dividing the budget into two parts, however, meant that we did not know how much each programme was costing us, or how strong or weak we were in financial terms: for example, whether Projekta would be able to continue its work if the Dutch funding ended.

A few years ago, we decided to introduce 'activity-based costing' into our budgeting and accounting. This tries to combine both programme costs and core costs. When the annual budget is prepared, we estimate the total core costs and divide them between the programmes, in proportion to staff hours worked on each programme.

The programme budgets that we offer to donors then show all their costs. If donors give us a fixed percentage of the proposed budget to help to cover administrative costs, we put it into a budget line from which we pay charges for rent, telephone, and transportation, plus core staff salaries, in fact all costs not directly relating to programme activities.

Even if a donor is not willing to contribute towards covering core costs, we still go ahead with the programme. We rely on our own fund-raising, sometimes by taking on an external consultancy which brings in money and contributes towards the missing amount of core costs.

Activity-based costing gives us better information on the full cost of each programme and helps us to fund them all. Most importantly, we can keep control of our costs. If they are too high, it alerts us to look for cheaper alternatives.

(Stichting Projekta, Surinam)

Box 21: Core costs – common concerns

Concerns	Possible solutions
None of our donors will fund core costs.	Make sure that any core costs which directly relate to a programme are budgeted and charged to that programme. Look for donors who will at least add a percentage towards your core costs. Ask the leadership team to decide how to fund these costs, considering the five ways shown earlier in this chapter.
Our donors already give a percentage for 'administration', so they will not cover any other core costs.	Talk to your donors to find out exactly what the administration percentage covers. Consider all your costs carefully and make sure your split between 'programme' and 'core costs' is accurate. See if any of your 'core costs' relate directly to the programme. For example, telephone costs may be charged to core costs in the budget, but in reality many of the calls, and a proportion of the rental charge, benefit the programme directly. Add in any costs to the programme budget that are not covered by the administration percentage.
All our funding is restricted. Although our donors give us an 'administration allowance', it is not enough to fund our core costs.	See if any of your costs can be reduced and whether you could raise any 'unrestricted' funds yourself, to help to fund the difference.
Our donor wants to know why we have included some core costs in the programme budget.	Tell the donor that you have included the full cost of the activity in the programme budget. This includes a proportion of the costs of running the organisation. Explain how your organisation works, and that it only exists to provide its activities (if this is true). If there were no activities, you would not need any core costs.

Part 4 |Tools for Building Financial Management Capacity

11 | 'Toolkit' for financial management capacity-building

Now that we have considered a number of areas in which to build financial management capacity, we turn to possible ways to put the ideas into practice.

Capacity-building can often be a slow and messy process. Many organisations want a 'quick fix' – maybe a single training course – but it is rarely quite so easy. Every organisation is different, and your needs are probably unique. Your capacity-building needs must be fully understood, and then 'tailor-made'. Often a mixture of methods is needed.

Talk to staff and volunteers from other organisations and to your stakeholders, to find out what might be possible. Donors will often bring suggestions from other organisations that they know and will sometimes provide funding for initiatives too. Most donors agree that capacity-building is an excellent idea, but some are less willing to help you to put it into practice. If you can, work with donors who can help you to achieve what you want. Don't be afraid to state your needs clearly. If you need help to build capacity, consider bringing in people with the right skills from outside your organisation.

This 'toolkit' is offered for use with your group or organisation and others that you know. All of the approaches described below have already worked well elsewhere. You might want to use all of them, or none. That's fine. Use methods that work best in your situation – and invent your own. Most importantly, talk with the individuals and organisations whose capacity is being built, to find the most useful approaches.

Some of the tools suggested can be useful for every part of the organisation; others will be appropriate for specific situations. Some could be used in building the capacity of financial staff, others for programme staff, still others for the leadership team.

Building relationships and communication

Good relationships and communication are at the heart of any capacity-building initiatives. This is an on-going process, and all the other tools depend on it.

Good relationships are especially important between finance and programme staff. Good or bad relationships can directly affect the quality of the programme.

In smaller organisations, this relationship sometimes works well. There are only a few people, and they see each other regularly, and so it is possible to communicate easily. As organisations grow, and especially as they start to form departments, communication may become more difficult. To maintain good communication, it is important for senior management to show that finance has a high priority and that they are personally disciplined in their financial work.

Giving encouragement

Remember to be positive about what is good. Sometimes it seems hard to find positive things to say, but people are much more likely to respond to being praised than being criticised. Find their strengths and tell people how much you appreciate good practice that they are demonstrating. Having done this, identifying the areas that need further work is more likely to be accepted and acted upon.

Asking questions

A powerful way of helping people to build their own capacity is to ask questions. Not only will this help the questioner, but the people answering them start to think about the way they do things, and about possible changes. The best questions lead people to build their own financial management capacity, without needing any external support.

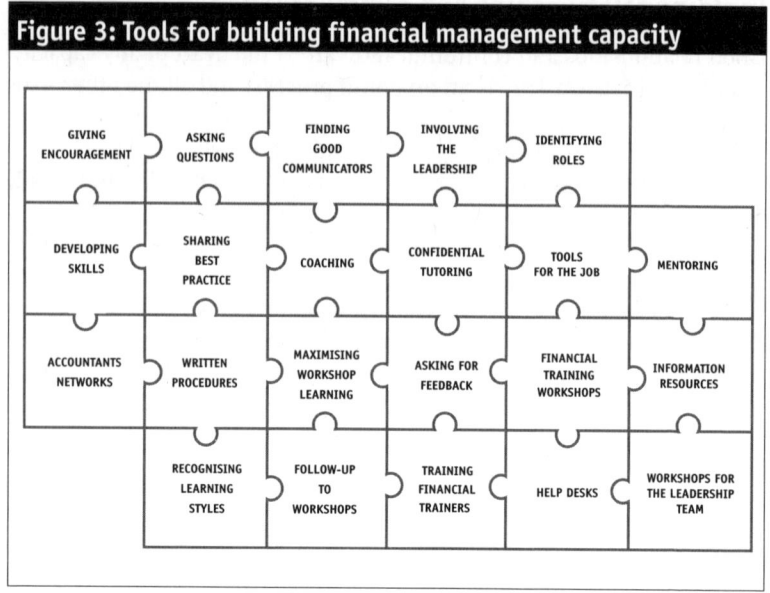

Figure 3: Tools for building financial management capacity

GIVING ENCOURAGEMENT	ASKING QUESTIONS	FINDING GOOD COMMUNICATORS	INVOLVING THE LEADERSHIP	IDENTIFYING ROLES
DEVELOPING SKILLS	SHARING BEST PRACTICE	COACHING	CONFIDENTIAL TUTORING	TOOLS FOR THE JOB	MENTORING
ACCOUNTANTS NETWORKS	WRITTEN PROCEDURES	MAXIMISING WORKSHOP LEARNING	ASKING FOR FEEDBACK	FINANCIAL TRAINING WORKSHOPS	INFORMATION RESOURCES
	RECOGNISING LEARNING STYLES	FOLLOW-UP TO WORKSHOPS	TRAINING FINANCIAL TRAINERS	HELP DESKS	WORKSHOPS FOR THE LEADERSHIP TEAM

Finding good communicators among finance staff

If you have good communicators among your finance staff, find
opportunities to involve them in communicating financial information
and funding issues with donors. These may be the people who can train
and support others. It is worth investing in their development, possibly as
financial trainers.

An example: The induction course for new staff included a session on
travel expenses. One member of the finance team was always keen to take
part. The training officer saw her potential and suggested that her skills
could be used more widely. The finance person developed one-to-one
financial training with the partner groups, which led to major
improvements in their accounting.

Building the leadership's capacity

Involving the leadership

Financial management capacity-building may fail if the leadership is
not involved. One solution may be to work with the leadership team first.
They can often become a catalyst for change in the organisation.
Such 'champions' might be, for example, the leader, a senior manager, or
a member of the management committee.

An example: The finance officer tried to improve financial management capacity by introducing new systems. The director did not see the point of this, and no progress was made. A new member of the management committee was appointed who had a background in accounting. The finance officer convinced him that change was needed in the systems. The new committee member acted as a 'champion' by talking with the leader and senior staff, and the new systems were successfully introduced.

Confidential tutoring

Confidential tutoring can help if the leader, or manager, does not know how to manage financially. Rather than admit to a lack of knowledge, this person may delegate everything, saying that the finance team can be trusted to do it all. He or she is unlikely to attend a training course, because it would mean 'losing face'. This lack of involvement is likely to result in poor systems and in major decisions being ill-informed. Eventually donors may stop funding because of the lack of good financial skills. If the issue is recognised, a possible solution is to arrange some confidential tutoring for the person concerned. The basics can be covered in a few sessions, and sometimes the tutor can then act as a mentor to the leader on financial issues.

Building staff capacity

Mentoring

What is mentoring?

The support of one individual by another on a regular basis. The aim is to empower the person being mentored to develop skills and build his or her confidence in dealing with unusual situations.

Someone with financial experience 'mentors' a member of staff. The mentor could be someone from the same or another organisation doing similar work. Mentors and 'mentees' often meet monthly, sometimes more regularly in the early stages. This is a good way of building the confidence of individuals within the organisation.

An example: Community-based organisations (CBOs) needed help in preparing their budget. The funding organisation's programme officer was able to prepare her own budget, but needed to develop confidence in teaching the CBOs how to do it. After she had worked with a mentor, she was able to support the CBOs in a practical way. An experienced mentor met her to give her support before and after each CBO visit.

Coaching

What is coaching?

Coaching is the 'use of one-to-one discussions to help a colleague find their own solutions using questioning, listening and feedback'.9

Coaching is a way of talking with people about how they can find solutions to work problems. It involves two people: the 'coach' and the 'coachee'. They meet on a regular, although sometime infrequent, basis. The coach has usually been trained to do this; it often needs no more than a day to learn the basics. Donors or commercial training organisations sometimes organise such training for coaches.

The coach does not need to know anything about finance in order to coach finance staff. Coaching is not about giving advice or being an 'expert'. It involves the coachees discovering the solutions themselves, and the coach being a facilitator to enable this to happen. Coaching builds financial management capacity by improving an individual's performance, confidence, and motivation. It increases staff retention, because people feel more valued. It can be used in many situations, with both finance and non-finance staff.

Sharing best practice

Members of staff have often worked elsewhere and seen good financial and management systems in place. Using best practice, they can help to professionalise their new organisation and other groups with which they work.

Building the capacity of the finance team

Developing the skills of finance staff

Finance staff skills can be developed by others within their organisation, or by an outside facilitator. First assess the gap between what is needed and what they are able to do, and decide whether 'on the job' training would help.

It might be helpful to organise exchange learning visits between the finance people from two organisations or, if the organisation is large enough, between two departments within the same organisation. Donors can sometimes help to identify (and possibly fund) suitable organisations.

An example: An organisation saw finance as a 'policing' role: making sure that other staff always used the right budget and that expenditure was correctly authorised. The accounts were always excellent. Another organisation saw the accounting role as 'enabling': making sure that programme staff achieved the results they wanted, by finding ways of doing things that sometimes contravened procedures. Both ways had advantages, and by bringing these organisations together to exchange ideas, valuable learning took place.

Identifying roles for finance staff

Finance staff may be unsure what is expected of them: whether they are employed simply to keep records, or something more.

Smaller organisations cannot usually afford highly trained finance staff, but the role still needs to be clarified so that staff can develop their skills and provide the best service to their organisation. In larger organisations, qualified accounting staff often say that managers do not make the best use of their skills. Qualified accountants, for example, are trained to take part in long-term decision-making, as well as undertaking their financial role. Staff may leave if their roles are not made clear and are not fulfilling their personal needs and potential.

Accountants' networks

In some countries, accountant networks for non-profit organisations are well established. If not, they can sometimes be introduced, either nationally or locally, by bringing together finance staff from different organisations. It works best if there is a specific reason for the meeting, for example a change in national regulations. This will encourage people to attend. The long-term benefit is often that participants will keep in touch and call on each other to discuss professional issues.

'Tools for the job'

Your finance staff need appropriate tools for their job. Tools vary according to circumstances: from small organisations needing a few hand-written records, to large organisations building a customised, computerised accounting system. As an organisation grows, its needs change and it should review and upgrade its tools.

An example: A small organisation had relied on a few hand-written records, but now it was receiving external funding. The records were not detailed enough to provide donor reports. This was the time to start using a computer spreadsheet programme with simple formats to keep the accounts and produce reports, both to the donor and to the organisation's management committee and managers. Someone from a local organisation offered to train staff in using computer spreadsheets.

Story: Tools for the job

The former co-ordinator was concerned that his NGO could not access the financial information needed to run the organisation and monitor its activities. He became critical of the book-keeper and said that she should be dismissed. The book-keeper was annoyed at the constant criticisms and misunderstandings, because she felt that she was doing her best to provide what she could with very limited resources.

To improve her own performance, the book-keeper then asked for support from the main donor's finance officer. She was introduced to simple tools for keeping accounts and preparing and monitoring the budget. The book-keeper worked with these tools, and the donor made follow-up visits, over a year or so. This helped to boost the book-keeper's confidence and helped her to identify her own position within the wider accounting role of the organisation. She felt encouraged to keep up-to-date information, provide the required information to other staff in the organisation, and give financial advice to their beneficiaries.

The book-keeper is now a key person in the organisation. She even feels able to challenge the new co-ordinator. She has put the organisation in a strong financial position to approach other donors for funding. The new director and staff are delighted that the book-keeping role has been clarified, and that the tools are now available to provide the financial information required.

(Agir Autrement pour le Développement en Afrique, Senegal)

Building resource capacity

Written financial procedures

Small organisations often operate without writing down how to do things, because everyone knows what to do. As organisations grow, they employ more people, and no one person can remember everything. At this point, systems are usually written down. This helps to build financial management capacity. The writer has to think through and develop the systems; the information is then available for everyone to refer to; and new staff and volunteers have access to the information.

However, there may be limits to this. For example, an organisation may distribute its written procedures but find it hard to understand why no one reads them. They may use technical jargon, may be badly written, or may be too long. Or it may simply be that the people for whom they were intended do not learn through reading (especially if the documents are written in their second language).

Some organisations find it useful to provide instructions about financial procedures on a 'need to know' basis. When the budgeting process starts, for example, this section of the procedures is circulated. The aim is to receive the right information, at the right level, at the right time. Other organisations communicate their basic procedures in a visual and/or verbal presentation at a group meeting. It is important to make sure that any who do not read or write are not left out. These meetings allow the issues to be discussed and questions to be raised by the people who will use them.

Information resources

Much general financial information is available in written and electronic formats. There is a list of resources in the 'Further reading' and 'Websites' sections towards the end of this book. Staff should be encouraged to use these and other resources for self-development. Make sure that the resources are easily available to all staff and not just kept in the leader's office.

Smaller organisations cannot always afford to buy printed or electronic resources. Donors will often offer specific funding for this purpose, if an item is entered in the budget. Talk to your donor about this.

'Help desks'

Large organisations sometimes offer a telephone or email 'help desk' for financial queries within their organisation. Donors sometimes provide smaller organisations with a similar service; for example, there may be a formal or informal arrangement with their donor's accountant.

Asking for feedback

Being open to feedback from others is a useful way of building financial management capacity. The feedback may come from members of the group, beneficiaries, other staff, volunteers, and donors. It may also come from formal reviews, for example an evaluation or audit. Feedback needs to be taken seriously: decide how valid the suggestions are and then, if appropriate, try them out.

An example: An organisation asked for feedback about the financial services provided during two weeks each year. There was a written questionnaire with three simple questions, which some people completed. Most feedback was gathered verbally when people came to the office. At the end of the two weeks, the information was gathered together and presented to a meeting of staff. Suggestions for improvements were then followed up.

12 | Training for financial management capacity-building

Training is often used as a method of capacity-building. This chapter considers how to use financial training; the use of follow-ups to workshops; how we might maximise the learning; and how we might train finance staff to become trainers themselves.

Capacity-building with financial training workshops

Training workshops provide an input for a larger group of people than would be possible with 'on the job' training. Participants meet people who do similar work in other organisations.

Workshops can be organised and funded by donors for a number of their partners. They can also be run by organisations internally and for their community groups, or by 'umbrella' groups for other non-profit organisations. Box 22 gives some guidance on the use of workshops.

Participatory training approaches (which actively involve participants in the training, rather than just talking at them) are essential for training in financial subjects. Courses should provide 'hands-on' experience of the task to be learned. The trainer should provide a programme describing what the course aims to cover and clear, well-written support materials for people to take away. If you are inviting outside speakers to take part in the training, check beforehand that they too will present their material in a participatory way.

For non-literate groups, use diagrams, verbal and visual activities, and objects to give the quantity and value that you want to show participants. If it is essential to have some things written down, it may be possible for participants to invite a literate relative or friend to accompany them.

Box 22: Thinking of using a workshop to build financial management capacity?

GREEN – go ahead

- If you have fully assessed the training needs.
- If the members of the group have similar backgrounds and experience.
- To increase the profile of finance within the organisation(s).
- To encourage senior managers and management committee members to develop financial management capacity-building skills.
- To encourage non-finance people to use financial management skills.
- To develop the skills of finance staff.

AMBER – be careful

- If you haven't first considered other approaches to financial management capacity-building.
- If the workshop is not really relevant to the needs of the participants.
- If the facilitator cannot use participatory training methods.

RED – don't proceed

- If you think a workshop will solve all your problems.
- If you expect that it will simply make people do what you want them to.
- If other approaches to financial management capacity-building will work better.

People who attend financial training may feel threatened by the process. It may remind them of school mathematics lessons. They may fear looking foolish. Trainers have to work hard to reassure course participants, and they should be positive, not critical, in their approach. Tell participants that you will always start off with the basics and use a step-by-step approach – and then do so.

Use simple formats for examples, remembering that people will often be seeing them for the first time. Once they are familiar with these formats, you can go on to slightly more complex examples. If possible, don't use technical language; but if you do use any, explain it first. Box 23 offers some guidelines to facilitators of financial training workshops.

Box 23: Facilitating financial training workshops

Do

- Prepare thoroughly.
- Be realistic about what is possible in the time available.
- State the purpose of each session.
- Deliver financial training with energy and enthusiasm.
- Start off each topic with the basics.
- Follow a logical pattern.
- Give out written materials to support the sessions.
- Get the group doing things – don't talk too long.
- Ask, and invite, questions.
- Encourage participants – be positive.
- Use a variety of methods – and have fun!

Don't

- Try to guess what the group already knows. If unsure, ask them.
- Use technical terms unless you first explain them.
- Rush the presentation.
- Try to cover everything.
- Make a participant feel that he or she has failed.

Make sure that financial workshops are open to all parts of the communities or organisations with which you work. Financial tasks can be done by a wide variety of people, but most need support and training to help them to achieve their full potential and benefit their community or organisation.

The outcome of workshops should be that participants feel more confident about the financial work of the organisation, and about their role within it. Also, after the workshop a much better relationship often develops between participants and the finance people who have facilitated such learning.

Follow-up to workshops

The best workshops include some follow-up by the facilitator. This is especially important for participants from smaller organisations. If, for example, the workshop is about basic accounting records, a visit to see how the participants are getting on and to give individual advice would be particularly helpful, about a month or so after the workshop.

This follow-up may lead to further visits or to mentoring participants.

Follow-up of learning can be more effective than a one-off workshop, because it makes sure that the learning is fully understood. It can be expensive, but some larger organisations or donors are willing to fund follow-up activities.

Story: Training and follow-up

Training for organisations needs more than a one-off course. The Copperbelt Health Education Project (CHEP) provides workshops for its beneficiaries in basic financial skills, resource mobilisation, and management of income-generating activities. The financial workshops cover topics such as completing accounting documents and cash/bank books, preparing bank reconciliations, and compiling financial reports to donors.

At the end of each workshop, the participants complete an action plan of tasks to carry out when they return to their organisation. During the meeting to review the action plan after the workshop, CHEP's staff check progress on agreed tasks – for example: 'Establishing an equipment register in the format taught during the training'. CHEP staff follow up this training with 'mentoring' and 'monitoring' visits to each of the participants.

The mentoring visit usually takes place two weeks after the course or workshop. It aims to discover whether the training has been effective in the participant's work situation. A typical visit would check that documentation exists for every stage of ordering goods. The community-based organisations (CBOs) are helped to develop project proposals. CBOs are also taught how to manage small business initiatives to contribute to their organisation's sustainability.

After the first mentoring visit, there are follow-up 'monitoring' visits to make sure that things are running smoothly. Further visits and telephone and email contact are then arranged for as long as needed.

(Copperbelt Health Education Project, Zambia)

Maximising workshop learning

All workshops should be used as an opportunity to pass on learning to others. Not only is this helpful for those who did not attend, but it reinforces the learning for those who did.

One of the most useful approaches is to develop the practice of requiring each participant to report back to their team what they have learned. This can be a brief report of the main highlights, supported, if possible, by materials copied for others to see. Workshop organisers can encourage this practice by including the question 'How will you pass this learning on to others?' on evaluation forms.

Some organisations send two people to financial training sessions, for example the leader and the finance person. Both benefit, and it also helps to provide continuity if later one of them leaves the organisation.

Different learning styles

It is sometimes assumed that everyone learns in the same way. This is not true. If the information that you want to share is important, plan to present it in different ways that will reach everybody, whatever their preferred learning style. Don't assume that everyone learns in the same way that you do! In some cultures, it is more natural to learn face to face than through the written word. The best way is to ask those involved 'How do you prefer to learn?'

Some of the different ways of acquiring new skills are listed below:

- 'on the job' training
- written information
- face-to-face instruction and discussions
- by teaching someone else
- participation in external courses, whether at a college, or by means of distance-learning or e-learning through the Internet
- short training sessions (as part of regular work meetings, perhaps)
- networking with other people doing similar work
- interactive computer packages.

Financial workshops for senior managers and management committee members

Workshops for the leadership team are less usual, but they can be an effective way of making change happen. If other methods of financial management capacity-building have not worked, it is worth asking if training at this level would help.

The leadership and management committee members are busy people, so it is important to limit the time involved to one or two days – whatever is possible – which means prioritising the material. For management committee members, the training may need to be fitted into their regular meetings. It is especially important to get the best facilitator available.

Training financial trainers

Building financial management capacity relies on the skills of individuals. People with financial skills do not always have the skills to train others. It is important to invest in training staff as financial trainers, if this is part of their job, and especially if they have the potential to be good trainers. General courses in the training of trainers are widely available. Some specialist courses are available for finance trainers; they help to develop skills and focus on ways of communicating financial management in a participatory manner.

Appendix A | Minimum financial requirements for growing organisations

Each organisation is different. This table offers a summary of the additional systems that can be introduced at each stage of growth.

	Early life	Growing up	Adulthood	Maturity
Possible situation	Group of volunteers; no commitments beyond immediate work; local fund-raising; no donor funding; whole group acts as the management committee	A few paid staff, rented premises; few financial commitments; one donor; management committee formed	More paid staff; own premises, equipment, and vehicles; financial commitments to beneficiaries; several donors	Many paid staff, premises, vehicles, and equipment; financial commitments to partners; many donors
		Early life plus…	*Early life and growing up plus…*	*Early life, growing up, and adulthood plus…*
Planning and budgeting	• Decide objectives • A basic budget	• Detailed budget to suit donor's format • Cash-flow forecast • Budget and actual reports produced for management committee	• Detailed planning • Budgets for each donor and one for the whole organisation • Budget and actual reports for managers	• Long-term planning • An organisational budget, showing donor funding • Detailed reports available for management
Accounts record-keeping	• Cash transactions • Bank account • Agree own records with bank statement	• Paper-based or computer spreadsheet record-keeping	• Computerised accounting package • Advances/loans and other registers	• Custom-made accounting system • Non-finance staff have access to read-only computerised accounting records

Financial reporting	• Summary of money received and spent presented to meetings	• Donor reports • Annual accounting statements • Beneficiary reports	• Accounts showing restricted and unrestricted funds	• Detailed annual report and accounting statements
Financial controls	• Two signatories on cheques	• Basic controls	• Comprehensive financial controls • Written financial procedures	• Detailed financial controls throughout organisation
External audit	• Independent examination	• Financial audit	• Management audit	• Audit examines programme activities
Staffing	• Group member deals with the finances	• Administrator appointed • Professional accountant to prepare end-of-year accounts	• Book-keeper appointed	• Professional accounting staff
Things to think about	• How to raise more funds	• The need for reserves • What could go wrong	• Financial training for non-finance staff • A reserves policy • New ways of paying for core costs	• Possibility of refusing donor funding • Possible risks • Encouraging partner organisations to develop their financial systems

Appendix B | Review of financial systems

Notes on using the review

This review helps you to assess your organisation's financial systems and identify its strengths and weaknesses. A minimum standard is given for each question. The review is a way of identifying improvements that can be made to strengthen your financial and management capacity, rather than a way of judging the organisation.

- If you score many 1s and 2s, you are likely to need some urgent action, and possibly to call on outside help.
- If you score mostly 4s and 5s, you have good financial systems, but there may still be some matters needing attention.

The best person to complete the review is someone who knows the organisation well. He or she can offer comments on most questions, or at least know where to find the information. Some questions will need to be answered by a senior person who understands the management committee. It is important that answers are as honest as possible, telling what actually happens, rather than what you think should happen.

It works best if someone inside the organisation conducts the review, rather than someone from outside. However, an external facilitator who is helping to build capacity can introduce it, as long as there is enough trust between them and the organisation.

Not every question is appropriate for every organisation, and you can add your own questions at the end. Small voluntary community-based organisations, for example, may not need all the systems covered in the review.

As you go along, write down comments in the column headed 'Any action needed'. When you have finished the review, write down the action points as a checklist, with a date by which you want to achieve them. Send a copy to all concerned.

A downloadable copy of this review is available at www.johncammack.net (click on 'Resources').

Review of financial systems

For each question, circle the number that most closely matches the present situation.

1 = Never, or don't know   2 = Rarely   3 = Occasionally   4 = Sometimes   5 = Always

Compare the response with the 'minimum standard' and write down 'any action needed'.

Technical terms are **highlighted** and explained in the Glossary towards the end of this book.

Question	Rating					Minimum standard	Any action needed
A. PLANNING AND BUDGETING							
1. Is an annual budget prepared and approved by the management committee?	1	2	3	4	5	The budget is prepared after talking with staff/other stakeholders. The management committee approves it, and checks that confirmed income covers expenditure.	
2. Is the budget based on current objectives?	1	2	3	4	5	The budget is based on current objectives.	
3. Do all relevant staff/volunteers discuss the budget details?	1	2	3	4	5	Relevant staff/volunteers are consulted about and/or contribute to budget discussions. Smaller organisations may include all their staff/volunteers.	
4. Are budgets finalised before the start of the financial year/project period?	1	2	3	4	5	The process is started early enough for it to be ready before the year/project starts.	

Question	Rating					Minimum standard	Any action needed
5. Are notes added to the budget, justifying items and showing calculations?	1	2	3	4	5	The person responsible for the budget adds notes.	
6. Does the budget avoid having more expenditure than income, unless this is planned?	1	2	3	4	5	If the budget shows that a deficit is likely, budgeted expenditure is reduced until more income is raised.	
7. Is a **cash-flow forecast** prepared, especially when there is not enough money?	1	2	3	4	5	A forecast is prepared regularly, and every time funds may run out. Best practice is to prepare a forecast which is updated each month.	
8. Do the management committee and leader regularly review a summary of the **budget and actual statement?**	1	2	3	4	5	Management committee regularly review the budget and actual statement. They ask questions about large differences between budget and actual figures.	
9. Do managers regularly review their expenditure/income against budget?	1	2	3	4	5	Managers review the budget and actual statement monthly/quarterly to make sure they are spending within budget.	
10. Are explanations for large differences between budget and actual noted on the budget and actual statement?	1	2	3	4	5	The person managing the budget writes notes on the budget and actual statement to explain large differences.	

Question	1	2	3	4	5	
11. Are budget and actual reports produced quickly after the period-end?	1	2	3	4	5	Budget and actual statements are produced within two weeks of the period-end. The management committee/ leader/manager can then act quickly.
12. Are meetings held between finance people and managers to discuss the contents of the budget and actual report?	1	2	3	4	5	Meetings, either one-to-one or in a group, are held immediately after the information is produced.
B. ACCOUNTS RECORD-KEEPING 1. Is the record of transactions (the **cash/bank book**) updated regularly?	1	2	3	4	5	The cash/bank book is updated daily, or whenever money is paid in or out. An up-to-date balance can always be calculated.
2. Is every cash/bank book entry supported by, for example, an invoice or receipt?	1	2	3	4	5	Documents are kept and filed. If there is no external document, a **payment voucher** is written, showing the details, which a more senior person approves.
3. Are financial documents filed in order?	1	2	3	4	5	Separate files are kept for money received and money paid. Documents are cross-referenced to the cash/bank book.
4. Is money received banked as soon as possible?	1	2	3	4	5	Money is banked as often as possible, depending on how much and how close the bank is.

Question	Rating					Minimum standard	Any action needed
5. Is a separate register kept, listing money given as a **cash advance** or as a loan to staff?	1	2	3	4	5	A **cash advances/loans register** lists all advances/loans and records when they are issued, accounted for, and repaid. It can easily show amounts outstanding, to be followed up. Loan repayments are deducted from salaries.	
6. Do the accounting records show donor funds given for a particular purpose?	1	2	3	4	5	Accounting records clearly show if funds are restricted. If funding is complicated and/or there are several donors, an extra system makes sure that **restricted funds** are monitored accurately.	
7. Is there a record to make sure that money due is all received and is on time?	1	2	3	4	5	Extra accounting records show money due and when it is paid, even if only in a notebook.	
8. Is a list of budget codes used to prepare the budget, and charge expenditure correctly?	1	2	3	4	5	The list of codes may be given by a computerised accounting package or by a donor. It may need to be customised.	
9. Is cash kept securely?	1	2	3	4	5	There is a safe or locked cupboard. No more cash is kept than is needed.	
10. Is the cash balance monitored?	1	2	3	4	5	Someone takes action when the cash balance becomes too low.	

Question	1	2	3	4	5	
11. Is a pre-numbered receipt issued for cash received?	1	2	3	4	5	Receipts are pre-numbered and show the organisation's name. The original is given to the person paying in the cash, and a copy is kept.
12. Does someone other than the cashier authorise payments?	1	2	3	4	5	The cashier only pays with authorised documents.
13. Does a senior person count the cash regularly?	1	2	3	4	5	A senior person agrees the cash balance with the cash/bank book at least weekly (on a different day each week).
14. Are bank accounts registered in the organisation's name?	1	2	3	4	5	All accounts are in the name of the organisation/ project.
15. Is there a separate cash/bank book for each bank account?	1	2	3	4	5	There is a **cash/bank book** for each bank account.
16. Has each bank account at least two signatories?	1	2	3	4	5	Each account has at least two people to sign cheques. If they are sometimes unavailable, more people will be needed.
17. Are cheques and payment instructions signed by two people?	1	2	3	4	5	Two people sign each cheque/payment instruction. This prevents errors and theft.
18. Are cheques signed after the details are entered?	1	2	3	4	5	'Blank' cheques should never be signed.

Question	Rating					Minimum standard	Any action needed
19. Is a **bank reconciliation** prepared every time a statement is received or the pass book updated?	1	2	3	4	5	A bank reconciliation is completed regularly, to agree the bank statement with the cash/bank book.	
20. Does the leader/manager approve the bank reconciliation?	1	2	3	4	5	The leader or a manager approves the bank reconciliation.	
21. Are cheques used as often as possible?	1	2	3	4	5	Cheques, not cash, are used whenever possible.	
22. Are cheque books kept securely?	1	2	3	4	5	Cheque books are kept in a safe or locked cupboard.	
23. Do cancelled cheques have 'cancelled' written on them, and are they kept for audit?	1	2	3	4	5	Cheques are cancelled when necessary, kept, and filed.	
24. Is there a list of all paid staff?	1	2	3	4	5	A staff list is kept up to date.	
25. Are staff taken off the payroll as soon as they leave?	1	2	3	4	5	There is a procedure for making sure no one can be paid after they have left. Someone other than the person responsible for paying the salaries checks this.	
26. Do staff sign for salaries received in cash?	1	2	3	4	5	Staff always sign a receipt when they receive a salary in cash.	

Question	1	2	3	4	5	
27. Are legal deductions calculated and paid to the appropriate authorities promptly?	1	2	3	4	5	Deductions required by law are made and paid when salaries are paid.
28. Are extra accounting records kept, for example ledger, journal, sales and purchase records, if needed?	1	2	3	4	5	Larger organisations need extra records, appropriate for their size/activities.
C. FINANCIAL REPORTING 1. Are annual **accounting statements** prepared, and do they show **restricted and unrestricted funds?**	1	2	3	4	5	Annual summaries of income and expenditure are produced. Larger organisations also have more detailed statements. They both show which funds are restricted for a particular use.
2. Do the management committee review and approve the annual accounting statements?	1	2	3	4	5	The management committee review and approve annual statements.
3. Can the accounting system produce donor reports in the required format?	1	2	3	4	5	Accounting systems produce donor reports in the required format.
4. Are donor reports always prepared on time?	1	2	3	4	5	Donor reports are prepared and sent on time.
5. Do donors receive a copy of the annual accounting statements?	1	2	3	4	5	There is a list of donors, and annual accounting statements are sent to donors and other stakeholders.
6. Are financial information and reports used to plan for the future?	1	2	3	4	5	Financial reports are used to plan future programmes.

Question	Rating					Minimum standard	Any action needed
D. FINANCIAL CONTROLS							
1. Are financial tasks separated?	1	2	3	4	5	No one person does the whole of any one financial transaction. This is to prevent errors and theft.	
2. Is expenditure authorised by a senior staff member (or the leader)?	1	2	3	4	5	Expenditure is approved before it is paid. Someone asks 'Where is it in the budget?'	
3. Are there limits on how much expenditure staff can authorise?	1	2	3	4	5	There are limits, and all staff, especially finance staff, know them.	
4. Do different people authorise payments and sign cheques for those payments?	1	2	3	4	5	No one person can authorise a payment and sign a cheque for the same transaction.	
5. Is there a list of authorised signatories, including their level of authorisation?	1	2	3	4	5	A signatories list is available.	
6. Are payments made only with an original invoice?	1	2	3	4	5	There is a system to avoid duplicate payments.	
7. Is the invoice checked against the original order, to help prevent double payment?	1	2	3	4	5	Purchase orders are attached to invoices, or a similar system is in place.	

	1	2	3	4	5	
8. Are several quotes asked for when making large purchases of goods or services?	1	2	3	4	5	Three quotes are required for goods or services (possibly only for items above a certain amount).
9. Does someone check that goods and services are received and in good condition before they are paid for?	1	2	3	4	5	The invoice is signed to show that the goods/services have been received and are of acceptable quality.
10. Is a record of what is owned (**fixed assets**) kept up to date and reviewed regularly?	1	2	3	4	5	A **fixed-asset register** is kept for details of items owned. This includes the date of purchase, the value, and where they were bought and are kept. This is agreed annually with the actual items.
11. Is there enough insurance to cover the current value of what is owned and for other risks?	1	2	3	4	5	Items owned are fully insured. Other risks (for example public liability, fire and theft, and cash in transit) should also be covered, if this is possible in the country where you work.
12. Can items be replaced easily when they wear out?	1	2	3	4	5	There is/will be funding to replace essential items.
13. Is everything owned kept securely?	1	2	3	4	5	Valuable items are locked or kept in locked rooms.
14. Is financial stationery numbered, named, and held securely?	1	2	3	4	5	All financial stationery is kept in a safe or locked cupboard.

Question	Rating					Minimum standard	Any action needed
15. Are the entrances to the premises and stores secured?	1	2	3	4	5	Premises should be locked and (if necessary) guarded.	
16. Is there a log book to record mileage for each vehicle?	1	2	3	4	5	Drivers should complete the vehicle log book each time a journey is made.	
17. Do staff pay for personal use of telephones and photocopiers?	1	2	3	4	5	Staff know the organisational policy and how to pay for use.	
18. Are a stock register and records kept?	1	2	3	4	5	There is a basic system of stock control, for example for drugs.	
19. Is stock counted regularly, and agreed with the stock register?	1	2	3	4	5	Stock counts are carried out by an independent person at least every three months.	
E. EXTERNAL AUDIT ASSESSMENT 1. Do the management committee select the auditors yearly?	1	2	3	4	5	Appointing the auditors is on the management committee's agenda each year.	
2. Does a **financial audit**/examination take place each year?	1	2	3	4	5	A yearly financial audit is conducted by an independent person/auditing firm.	
3. Is the audit firm (or individual auditors within the same firm) changed every four or five years?	1	2	3	4	5	The auditor firm, or the individual responsible within a firm, is replaced every four to five years.	

Question	1	2	3	4	5	
4. Does the auditor provide a letter giving recommendations?	1	2	3	4	5	The auditor makes recommendations (the 'management letter') to the management committee at the end of the audit.
5. Does the management committee see the auditor's recommendations and take the necessary action?	1	2	3	4	5	Recommendations are implemented and followed up.
6. Does the auditor provide a **management (or systems) audit?**	1	2	3	4	5	The auditor looks at financial and management systems and the use of management information.
F. MANAGEMENT COMMITTEE						
1. Does one member of the management committee take the lead on financial issues?	1	2	3	4	5	One member of the management committee is responsible for financial issues.
2. Can members of the management committee understand basic financial information, or are they being trained?	1	2	3	4	5	At least one other person, besides the lead finance person, is competent to ask questions about financial information at meetings.
G. FINANCE STAFF						
1. Are finance staff competent?	1	2	3	4	5	Finance staff have suitable training and/or experience.
2. Are job descriptions available for all finance staff?	1	2	3	4	5	All staff have job descriptions.

Question	Rating					Minimum standard	Any action needed
3. Are qualifications and references checked before new staff are appointed?	1	2	3	4	5	References and qualifications are always checked.	
4. Do interviewees take a practical test of their financial skills?	1	2	3	4	5	Tests are used to assess skills when candidates are interviewed for finance posts.	
5. Are staff encouraged to take further training?	1	2	3	4	5	Someone is responsible for encouraging staff development.	
6. Is the number/level of staff enough for the organisation's activities?	1	2	3	4	5	There are enough staff, especially when extra-large funding is received.	
7. Are some staff able to communicate effectively to a non-financial audience?	1	2	3	4	5	At least one person can explain financial information and its impact on the organisation.	
8. Is there continuity of staff?	1	2	3	4	5	There is enough continuity. If high turnover is due to low salaries, the leadership team should consider other ways of valuing/keeping staff.	
H. FINANCIAL INFORMATION 1. Is the information given to the management committee, leader, and managers up to date?	1	2	3	4	5	Information is available within two weeks of the period-end.	

Question	1	2	3	4	5	Notes
2. Is information presented in a user-friendly format?	1	2	3	4	5	The management committee receive a summary of the budget and actual statement; managers have a more detailed version.
3. Are financial policies and procedures put in writing?	1	2	3	4	5	Except for very small organisations, written procedures are available.

I. CULTURE

Question	1	2	3	4	5	Notes
1. Do the management committee prioritise financial matters at their meetings?	1	2	3	4	5	The management committee/senior staff receive regular financial reports at their meetings.
2. Does the leader prioritise finance and encourage everyone else to do the same?	1	2	3	4	5	Staff and volunteers know that high standards of financial management are expected.
3. Does the leader submit his/her financial forms quickly?	1	2	3	4	5	The leader sets an example.
4. Are programme staff and other staff aware of financial issues?	1	2	3	4	5	Staff are confident to do the financial tasks in their job description.
5. Is there a numerical test at interviews for non-finance staff who have financial responsibilities in their job description?	1	2	3	4	5	Numerical tests should be used to assess existing skills and/or show what training is needed.

Question	Rating					Minimum standard	Any action needed
J. EXTERNAL RELATIONSHIPS 1. Do the management committee and the leader consider external risks?	1	2	3	4	5	Time to consider what could go wrong is included in the yearly planning process.	
2. Is there a strong, transparent relationship with beneficiaries, donors, and other stakeholders?	1	2	3	4	5	The organisation, its beneficiaries, and donors can all obtain answers to their financial/general questions, in an open and friendly way.	
3. Do stakeholders trust the financial management?	1	2	3	4	5	Stakeholders trust the organisation's financial systems and staff.	
4. Do stakeholders (including beneficiaries) receive regular financial reports in a suitable format?	1	2	3	4	5	All stakeholders, including beneficiaries, receive appropriate information about financial aspects of the work.	
5. Do finance staff meet with beneficiaries to discuss financial matters?	1	2	3	4	5	Depending on the size and style of the organisation, finance staff and beneficiaries can talk with each other about financial matters.	
K. OTHER QUESTIONS 1. Is there a fund-raising plan?	1	2	3	4	5	A fund-raising plan has been adopted and implemented.	
2. Has the organisation got several sources of funds?	1	2	3	4	5	The organisation relies on more than one funding source.	

Question	1	2	3	4	5	Comments
3. If donor funding were to stop immediately, could the organisation continue until new funds were raised?	1	2	3	4	5	Enough funds are available to pay essential costs until new sources of income can be identified and money received.
4. Are donors' funds used only in accordance with their wishes?	1	2	3	4	5	A system for accounting for **restricted funds** is in place (see also question B6).
5. Has the organisation considered whether it needs a **reserves fund** and policy?	1	2	3	4	5	Reserves funds have been discussed. If they are needed, there are plans and a policy for establishing and maintaining them.
6. Is there a policy for funding **core costs?**	1	2	3	4	5	The management committee have considered this, although it may be difficult to find an ideal solution.
Your own questions						
	1	2	3	4	5	
	1	2	3	4	5	
	1	2	3	4	5	

Action points

Date of review of action points ....

Signed .... Date ....

Signed .... Date ....

Notes

1   Tools for Self Reliance (2005) *Tools for Self-reliance Annual Report*, Southampton: Tools for Self Reliance.

2   Adapted with permission from Environmental Support Center and Innovation Network (2002) *Echoes from the Field: Proven Capacity-building Principles for Nonprofits*, Washington: Environmental Support Center and Innovation Network, Inc., www.envsc.org www.innonet.org

3   CAMFED International (2004) *CAMFED Annual Review 2003/04*, Cambridge: CAMFED International.

4   John Cammack (2000), *Financial Management for Development*, Oxford: International NGO Training and Research Centre (INTRAC).

5   Reproduced with permission from 'Financial Management for Emergencies, a Survival Guide for Humanitarian Programme Managers', www.fme-online.org, © 2005 John Cammack, Timothy Foster, and Simon Hale.

6   Caroline Clark (2001) *Managing Risk*, London: National Council for Voluntary Organisations.

7   Charity Commission (2005) *Accounting and Reporting by Charities: Statement of Recommended Practice*, London: Charity Commission.

8   Bill Bruty (2005) 'Guidance Notes: Core Funding Strategies', www.bond.org.uk (click on 'Publications/Assessing funding opportunities'); based on research by Mike Hudson (1999) in *Managing without Profit*, London: Penguin Books.

9   Sian Richards (2005) 'ITC Coaching for Senior Managers', London: Independent Theatre Council (unpublished), www.sianrichards.com

Glossary

Accounting statements: financial summaries produced at the end of an accounting period. Examples: receipts and payments account, income and expenditure account, balance sheet.

Bank reconciliation: a statement confirming that accounting records agree with the bank statement or pass book.

Beneficiaries: people, groups, and communities who benefit from the activities and services provided by a non-profit organisation.

Budget and actual statement: a comparison of budgeted income and expenditure with actual income and expenditure, showing differences.

Cash advance: money given to an individual, usually a member of staff, for a work activity (for example travel) when precise details of the cost are not known.

Cash-advances/loans register: a record of money given to an individual. It shows if, and when, the amount was accounted for.

Cash/bank book: a record of money coming in and going out, in date order. 'Cash book' means both cash and bank transactions.

Cash-flow forecast: a statement which forecasts the money coming in and going out over a period of time in the future.

Champion: someone who promotes ('champions') a particular issue in a group or organisation; for example, a member of the leadership team.

Community-based organisations (CBOs): small non-profit groups, sometimes run entirely by volunteers, based in the community that they serve.

Core costs: non-programme costs of an organisation. Sometimes called overheads or support costs.

Financial audit: an examination of financial records and statements.

Financial management: the use of financial information, skills, and methods to make the best use of an organisation's resources.

Financial management capacity: an organisation's financial management, awareness, competence, and relationships which are used to make its overall management and programme activities effective.

Fixed assets: items owned for more than one year. Examples: buildings, vehicles, and computers.

Fixed-asset register: a list of fixed assets, updated regularly.

Leader: the person responsible for the organisation's activities. He or she may be the chair of the management committee or, in larger organisations, a senior staff member, sometimes called the Director.

Leadership team: the management committee, leader, and senior staff of a group or organisation.

Management audit (or systems audit): an examination of an organisation's management and financial processes and systems.

Management committee: the body responsible for the management of a group or organisation who meet regularly to decide policies. The committee may also be called the advisory body, board, executive committee, governing body, or trustees. In small non-profit organisations the whole group may constitute the committee; in larger organisations the committee is sometimes made up of representatives of the membership.

Managers: people responsible for a particular activity, department, or project. They usually have responsibility for the budget and staff.

Non-government organisations (NGOs): non-profit organisations, usually with paid staff and volunteers. They vary in size and may be locally or nationally based.

Organisation: people working together in the non-profit sector for social objectives. It can be any size, from a small community group to a large national or international agency.

Partners: two or more organisations working together for a common purpose. A donor is often one of the partners.

Payment voucher: a document attached to an invoice or receipt, to record details of payments.

Programme staff: staff working for a community-based organisation, non-government organisation, or charity, on activities with social objectives. In larger organisations, these staff might be advising or working with their 'partner' organisations.

Reserves: organisational savings held to cover future shortages in funding and emergencies.

Restricted funds: money received from a donor for a particular purpose.

Stakeholders: groups and individuals, internal or external, who have an interest in the organisation's well-being. They include beneficiaries, community groups, partners, volunteers, staff, government, donors, suppliers, and the wider public.

Umbrella group: an organisation co-ordinating and representing non-profit organisations, often nationally.

Unrestricted funds: money that can be used for any expenditure within the organisation or project.

Websites

British Overseas NGOs for Development (Bond)
'Guidance notes' on capacity-building topics, including budgeting and core costs
www.bond.org.uk (click on 'Publications/International programme
work/Assessing funding opportunities')

Capacity.org
Resources for capacity-building (English, French, and Spanish)
www.capacity.org

Civicus
'Toolkits' for capacity-building (English, French, Spanish, and Russian)
www.civicus.org/new/content/toolkits1.htm

Financial Management for Emergencies
A survival guide for humanitarian programme managers
www.fme-online.org

Gender Budgeting
What it is, what it is not, and how it can be used in non-government organisations
www.johncammack.net (click on 'Resources')

Global Development Network
Tips and suggestions for applying for funds and proposal writing
www.gdnet.org (click on 'Online services/Toolkits')

International NGO Training and Research Centre (INTRAC)
Resources for organisational capacity-building (English and French)
www.intrac.org (click on 'Praxis programme')

John Cammack
Extra resources for this book, useful research, and web links
www.johncammack.net

Management Accounting for NGOs (Mango)
Accounting and financial resources
www.mango.org.uk

NGO Support Toolkit
Resources for assessing organisational capacity (for downloading)
www.ngosupport.net

Plain English Campaign
Advice on clear communication and tips
www.plainenglish.co.uk (click on 'Free guides and software')

Progressio
'Capacity Building for Local NGOs: a Guidance Manual for Good Practice'
www.ciir.org (click on 'Publications')

Thiagi Group
Free games for participatory training
www.thiagi.com (click on 'Free resources')

Further reading

Accounting and financial management

Cammack, J. (2000) *Financial Management for Development: Accounting and Finance for the Non-specialist in Development Organisations*, Oxford: International NGO Training and Research Centre (INTRAC).

Cammack, J. (2003) *Basic Accounting for Small Groups, Second Edition with Exercises for Individual and Group Learning*, Oxford: Oxfam GB.

Collins, R. (1994) *Management Controls for Development Organisations Part 1 and 2*, Crediton: Stephen Sims and Partners.

Gupta, K. N. and M. Fogla (eds.) (2004) *Manual of Financial Management and Legal Regulations*, Delhi: Financial Management Services Foundation.

Sayer, K. (2007) *A Practical Guide to Financial Management*, London: Directory of Social Change.

Capacity-building

Crooks, B. (2003) *Capacity Self-assessment*, Teddington: Tearfund.

Eade, D. (1997) *Capacity-Building: An Approach to People-centred Development*, Oxford: Oxfam GB.

Core costs

Fiennes, C., C. Langerman, and J. Vlahovic (2004) *Full Cost Recovery: A Guide and Toolkit on Cost Allocation*, London: ACEVO and New Philanthropy Capital.

Holloway, R. (2001) *Towards Financial Self-Control*, London: Earthscan in association with Civicus and the Aga Khan Foundation.

Training

Chambers, R. (2002) *Participatory Workshops*, London: Earthscan.

Guijt, I., J.N. Pretty, I. Scoones, and J. Thompson (1995) *Participatory Learning and Action – a Trainer's Guide*, London: International Institute of Environment and Development.

Index

A indicates text in an appendix, B text in a box, and F text in a figure.